Teacher Induction and Mentoring

SUNY Series
EDUCATIONAL LEADERSHIP
Daniel L. Duke, editor

Teacher Induction and *Mentoring*

School-Based Collaborative Programs

Edited by
Gary P. DeBolt

With a Foreword by
Greta Morine-Dershimer

State University of New York Press

Published by
State University of New York Press, Albany

©1992 State University of New York

For information, address the State University of New York Press,
State University Plaza, Albany, NY 12246

Production by Bernadine Dawes
Marketing by Bernadette LaManna

Library of Congress Cataloging-in-Publication Data

1   2   3   4   5   6   7   8   9   10

*This work, and all my life, are dedicated to
my wife and friend, Gwen, who is my soul
and my inspiration.*

Contents

Part III: Lessons and Questions Evolving from Research and Practice

Preface

"Education . . . is not a bunch of tricks or even a bundle of knowledge. Education is something we neither 'give' nor 'do' to our students. Rather, *it is a way we stand in relation to them*" (Daloz, *Effective Teaching and Mentoring,* xv).

This book is about education. It is about seeking ways to improve education in general by improving the induction of new teachers. If the process of induction can be made less traumatic and destructive, perhaps we can reduce the extremely high attrition rates for teachers during their first five years. One of the most tragic aspects of high attrition is the loss of many of our most promising new teachers. The use of experienced, successful teachers to mentor new teachers is one way to improve the induction of new teachers and, hopefully, to reduce the loss of promising teachers. This book is also about education for those interested in learning about mentoring.

Mentoring can have many definitions and can take many forms. This book provides: (a) an overview of the induction into teaching and mentoring processes; (b) descriptions of five school-based collaborative models of mentoring projects; and (c) an examination of lessons and questions evolving from research and practice regarding the mentoring of new teachers.

Overview of the Book

The book begins with a foreword, written by Greta Morine-Dershimer, which describes how this work fits into the larger picture of research on teaching and teacher education. As a recent vice-president of the American Educational Research Association, Morine-Dershimer has a broad perspective of the knowledge base of teaching and the need for case studies to describe what is being done in the schools.

The book is divided into three parts. Part one establishes a broad theoretical basis for this work's examination of mentoring within the contexts of induction and the process of becoming a teacher. Chapter one will describe the induction process and the role of induction in the process of becoming a teacher. It will be followed by an examination of mentoring and its role within the broader context of induction.

Part two, including chapters three through seven, presents individual and varied models of mentoring programs for induction as they have been conceptualized and implemented in New Mexico, rural upstate New York, Arizona, New York City, and Northern Colorado. Each chapter begins with a headnote to identify key connections to the larger context outlined in chapters one and two. The uniqueness of each model is exciting. Through each chapter runs a common theme of how mentoring is viewed within the broader context of induction and how this perspective is reflected in that model of mentoring.

Chapters eight and nine, part three, provide a research report about items that classroom teachers view to be helpful in their work as mentors of new teachers. This section concludes with suggested lessons and questions that policymakers, administrators, and teachers might ask as they begin to plan for successful, effective mentoring projects in their schools. The final chapter draws some conclusions and generalizations from the entire work. It ends by raising questions that will likely be faced by policymakers, school administrators, and teacher educators as they continue to pursue ways of designing and implementing induction programs that incorporate mentoring of new teachers.

Collectively, the contributors to this book have reported experiences gained through practice and research. Their work represents a diverse sample of models of school district and university collaboration. Educators in a variety of positions can benefit from the experiences reported here as they begin to conceptualize, plan, and implement mentor programs to fit the unique set of contexts and resources found in their school setting.

This work is a "step along the path." It is neither the beginning nor the end. I hope this book will lead to useful questions and ideas for those responsible for making policy decisions. Policymakers and educational administrators are aware of the growth of mentoring programs. Educators will benefit from the case study format of the book, since it provides them with detailed information about a variety of mentoring programs. The text will help provide them with background knowledge of mentoring and alternative means of conceptualizing the process of supporting mentoring. Armed with such knowledge, and the questions raised by it, administrators might be better prepared to deal with the realities of translating the theories of mentoring into practice for their particular schools. Administrators need to be aware of potential benefits of mentoring for teachers, schools, children, and administrators themselves.

This book will also be helpful to those interested in the processes of becoming a teacher and of mentoring as part of that process. If becoming a teacher is viewed as a continuum, teacher educators and prospective mentor teachers will stand to benefit from this work. Just as specific instruction and support can enhance a teacher's effectiveness, so too can specific support and assistance improve an experienced teacher's ability to serve as a mentor of a new teacher. Awareness, instruction, and support are key issues in mentoring programs.

As educators, we must seek ways to enhance teachers' effectiveness both as new teachers and as mentor teachers. How can we encourage the development of their competence and performance in ways that will enable them to interpret and apply their knowledge and skills to new tasks and settings? Herein are a variety of examples of support programs to develop teacher and mentor competency and to facilitate their performance toward a goal of increased effectiveness. As noted by Huling-Austin (1989), programs to assist new teachers often strive to reach a variety of goals. Increased teacher effectiveness is but one of those goals; yet, it is a very important one. Other goals, which are not to be minimized, are to increase retention of good teachers; reduce the problems of the first year of teaching; support, both personally and professionally, the new teacher; socialize the new teacher; and satisfy mandates for induction.

I hope that reading this book will lead to questions about education—education for the children of our schools; teacher education; the education of mentor teachers; and their roles in the development of new teachers. In each facet of education, there is a relationship: teacher to student, teacher educator to preservice teacher, policymaker and administrator to mentor teacher, and mentor to new teacher. It is, in each situation, important to consider the "way we stand in relation" to each other. What lessons can we learn from those who have gone before us in this work of mentoring?

I wish to express my gratitude to the contributors to this work. They have been wonderful. Also, a special appreciation exists for Greta Morine-Dershimer's support and encouragement. She serves as a shining model for those of us who aspire to be good teachers and good teacher educators. Priscilla Ross has been an outstanding editor and teacher. She has guided me through the writing and publication processes with patience and skill. Finally, I wish to express my deep appreciation and respect for Dawn M. Rowe. She has skillfully typed and reviewed the many drafts of the entire work.

Gary P. DeBolt
June 1991

Foreword

Learning to teach involves the gradual acquisition of professional expertise over an extended period of time. Tracing the gradual acquisition of teaching knowledge and skill is not an easy matter. Influencing that acquisition in order to enhance the development of professional expertise is decidedly difficult. Yet both of these tasks are essential for the improvement of teaching and learning in our public schools. These are the tasks that mentoring and induction programs have undertaken. This book provides us with an opportunity to see the variety of ways that the tasks have been addressed by different programs and reveals some common concerns and useful outcomes of these programs.

Studies of teacher education have long been attentive to stages of development in learning to teach. Ways of conceptualizing these stages have changed over time, from Fuller and Bown's (1975) delineation of four stages of concerns, to Berliner's (1988) depiction of five stages of expertise. Mentoring and induction programs focus our attention on transitions from one stage of teacher development to another.

The transition from student to teacher is the most dramatic transition in learning to teach. The individual in this transition must change from thinking and acting as a student, absorbed with his or her own learning and performance, to thinking and acting as a teacher, accepting responsibility for the learning and performance of others. Beginning teachers are fully engaged in this critical transition, and mentoring programs are specifically designed to support them through this period of chance.

The transition from teacher to teacher educator is less well recognized as an important phase in learning to teach, but it is becoming a more prevalent transition as induction and mentoring programs have expanded in school districts throughout the nation. When experienced teachers serve as mentors for first-year teachers, they are required to become more aware of their own decisions and teaching behavior in order to explain their reasoning and actions to the novices with whom they work. In addition, new skills and knowledge related to working with adult learners are needed. It is not universally recognized that mentor teachers need special support as they engage in their new roles. The programs described in this volume address this issue.

A few mentoring programs assist individuals in a third type of transition. These are experienced teachers who are working in a new instructional context (e.g., new to the district, new to a grade level, new to a subject matter area). To the extent that any change in the context for teaching requires the development of new knowledge, skills, or attitudes, these changes create another important transition in learning to teach. This is a type of transition experienced by large numbers of teachers, but it is a transition period for which there has been almost no support provided in most schools. Induction programs may lead to a greater awareness of the need to assist teachers in this type of transition.

The cases presented here do more than alert us to the importance of these three types of transitions in learning to teach; they portray the variation that is possible in the design of programs intended to support teachers in these transitions. The programs vary in

1. length of experience—the University of Northern Colorado began their program in 1973; Hunter College began theirs in 1987.

2. beginning teacher to mentor ratio—the East Harlem/
Hunter College program has a one to one or two to one ratio;
the Albuquerque Public Schools/University of New Mexico
program has a sixteen to one ratio.

3. the type of beginning teachers served—the Hunter
College program focuses on minority teachers; the University
of Northern Colorado program includes teachers who are reentering the profession after a time-out period.

4. the specificity of training provided for mentors—the
Arizona State University/Maricopa County Schools program
provides intensive training in use of a specific assessment instrument, as well as in observation and coaching; mentors in
the University of Northern Colorado program participate
with beginning teachers in joint graduate seminars, led by
University personnel.

Despite this variety in program design, the mentoring programs
described here share some common concerns. These include mentors' role definitions (most agree that they should assist, but not assess
new teachers); and mentors' characteristics (most agree that the selection process is critical to program success). Furthermore, all of
these programs have made some effort to document or evaluate program outcomes. The most useful form of documentation reveals that
mentoring programs have contributed to improved retention of beginning teachers. Another desirable outcome involves increased collaboration between school districts and universities in the design and
implementation of these programs.

An important strength of this book is the use of these varied cases
to assist the reader in perceiving the possibilities that exist for shaping
a mentoring program to fit the needs of a particular situation. The in-
troductory chapters set a broader context for the cases: highlighting
the important functions to be served by induction programs (chapter
1); and providing an interesting historical perspective on the concept
of "mentor" (chapter 2). The concluding chapters draw together the
lessons to be learned from these cases: presenting the views of experienced mentors about how to improve the services provided by

these programs (chapter 8); and summarizing the issues still to be resolved and questions yet to be answered (chapter 9).

Too frequently, those of us engaged in educational reform movements have been so busy implementing new programs that we have failed to document program operations or evaluate program outcomes. The cases presented here provide us with a good set of models, not only by their varied adaptations to particular settings, but by their attention to documentation. There is much to be learned here.

Greta Morine-Dershimer

Part I

Theoretical Basis

Mentoring does not operate in isolation. It builds upon a complex set of contexts in which teachers live and work. Chapter 1 sets the process of mentoring within the context of teacher induction and provides a theoretical basis for such programs. The second chapter examines the literature of mentoring of new teachers.

1.

The Place of Induction in
Becoming a Teacher

GERALD M. MAGER

Tom Tyker never beat me up. While other boys in that third grade
class cowered in the presence of this older boy, I was at ease. We
had an understanding, Tom and I, born of the lunchtimes we spent
together while others were on the playground. As a good student,
I was to guide him through the math and reading and spelling he
hadn't learned. I was the means by which our teacher gave him
some extra help. And, I suppose, the review sessions kept him away
from others, out of trouble. For some reason, he never bullied me.

I don't know whether Tom ever learned any math or reading
or spelling during those lunchtimes. And in fifth grade he got into
trouble for the last time and was kicked out of our school. But my
recollection of those days suggests to me that it was with Tom
that I started to become a teacher. With no knowledge of methods, with motives that were supplied, with effectiveness measured
only in the plaudits of our teacher and the witness of other students, I began to see the possibility of myself as a teacher.

(The reflections of a teacher, on becoming one.)

"Becoming a Teacher" Revisited

In their now classic chapter in the 1975 NSSE Yearbook, *Teacher Ed-
ucati on,* Frances Fuller and Oliver Bown explored the experience of

3

"Becoming a Teacher" as it was reflected in the extant empirical literature on learning to teach. They first considered the context in which one becomes a teacher, and then addressed the experience itself. It was in this latter section that they put forth the idea that individuals who become teachers pass through stages of concerns as they learn to teach.

According to this concerns-based model of becoming a teacher, preservice teachers move from concern about their own survival as classroom teachers, to concern about the situations in which they are expected to teach, to concern about pupils. This view of becoming a teacher matches what many teacher educators have observed as they work with prospective teachers. It has become a classic view of the progression of changes in teacher candidates.

Perhaps because this concerns-based model had become so widely recognized and valued, the words *becoming a teacher* are often associated primarily with the steps of preservice teacher preparation. Such an association, however, misses a point made by several researchers and which Fuller and Bown themselves reiterate in the very same chapter: The experience of learning to teach does not begin with a preservice preparation program, but rather begins earlier in one's experience as a child and student. These early influences are important bases of motivations and choices made in entering a teaching career and beginning practice. Furthermore, the authors suggest, after preservice preparation, the experience of becoming a teacher continues into the inservice years of a teacher's career. A teacher continues to learn about teaching as the practice is carried out.

If one were to revisit Fuller and Bown's chapter, and the many subsequent reports in the literature on teacher education and teaching, the words *becoming a teacher* would most certainly be given a broader reading than simply the experience of preservice preparation.

What Is It to Become a Teacher?

Becoming a teacher has elements of building a self-image. The teacher whose experience with Tom Tyker is recollected above might well mark that experience as the start of his becoming a teacher. Other teachers have similar stories to report about events which marked the starts of their careers.

More traditionally, when a preservice teacher completes a program of study and has been granted a teaching credential, he or she has "become a teacher." This step of becoming has an element of image-building—seeing oneself as legitimate. But it also has related elements of qualification and capacity—having knowledge, skills, and values necessary for teaching practice.

It might be argued by some that becoming a teacher means being hired to teach, being given an opportunity to practice as a teacher. This affirms the self-image and puts to use the acquired knowledge, skills, and values. It also particularizes those elements: at first, as related to content, grade level, school, and district; and eventually, as related to particular students, events, and circumstances. Thus, one becomes a teacher in the particular context in which one is hired to practice.

Research on teachers' careers suggests that the first three to five years of teaching are a period of time in which an individual moves from "novice" to "established" teacher status. In a sense, the new teacher continues to become a teacher throughout that period, acquiring contextually useful knowledge, skills, and values; and refining, detailing, and deepening the image of self-as-teacher.

Finally, it is not uncommon for veteran teachers to report that in some ways they are still becoming teachers—still creating their professional practice to respond to the needs and opportunities presented by each year and each student.

While all of these instances of becoming a teacher seem different, they have in common elements of developing an image of self-as-teacher, and acquiring knowledge, skills, and values upon which to base practice. Furthermore, these instances suggest that becoming a teacher is a highly personalized experience: in the least, the influence of experiences as a child and student make it different for each individual; the particulars of the context in which one begins and continues to practice teaching enhance those differences. Relatedly, they point to the importance of context in shaping the experience. Finally, these instances suggest that becoming a teacher is a continuum of experiences over a span of time, rather than one point in time.

To "become a teacher" might better be thought of as *the continuous experience of an individual through which an image of self-as-teacher is formed and refined, and during which knowledge, skills, and values appropriate to the work of teaching, as it is to be practiced in a particular context, are acquired and used.*

Teacher Preparation and Becoming a Teacher

If becoming a teacher is to be interpreted as more than engaging in a preservice preparation program, it is then useful to consider just what part preservice teacher preparation plays in the overall experience. In what ways does it add to the experience of becoming a teacher? How does it differ from other experiences that are part of that development?

Conventional and unconventional preparation. As already suggested, the experiences that individuals bring to teacher preparation programs vary as much as the people themselves. The motives they bring to the work of teaching; the beliefs and personal theories about what is effective; the images they hold of themselves—what kind of teacher they will be, what they will be good at, what will be their weaknesses: these are all matters that make one prospective teacher's entry into a program somewhat different from the next prospective teacher's. These matters will also make the unfolding experience of the program different for each individual.

Though there is great variance among the individuals who pursue teaching careers through preservice preparation, the program they enter (even though there are literally thousands of them) follow fairly conventional patterns. Indeed, because most if not all of these programs are designed to meet the requirements for registration with the various state education agencies, they might be characterized as "standardized." The match between an individual's unique experience of becoming a teacher and a program's contribution to that development may be good or it may be rough; the goodness of fit may be an important determinant of the success of the program in contributing to the individual's becoming a teacher.

The conventional preservice teacher education program is designed for a student who will enroll in a four-year college or university program which leads to a bachelor's degree and an initial credential for teaching. In the conventional program, a student begins with the general requirements of the institution and courses in the liberal arts and sciences. Often in the first and second years of undergraduate study, the professional education component is begun with courses that include early field experiences: a time when commitments to teaching can be confirmed or reexamined, and when learning about teaching becomes a process different from what has been experienced in all the years of being a student. The conventional program continues in the third and fourth years of undergraduate study with additional courses in liberal arts and sciences, typically including concentrated study in one field or in related interdisciplinary fields. The professional education component continues with more in-depth study of the foundations of education and of teaching methods and curriculum; often additional field experiences are incorporated into these professional studies. The conventional program concludes with an extended field experience—student teaching—which is typically considered the capstone of the program; teachers often report, retrospectively, that it was in student teaching that they learned how to teach.

An increasing number of individuals are beginning their pursuit of teaching as a career after their undergraduate years. These individuals may build on their undergraduate majors to form their content area specializations. Some of these individuals are coming to the work of teaching as a change of career, after years of success in another field. These prospective teachers often select preparation programs which extend undergraduate study or are combined with graduate study programs. Though they begin their professional studies at a point different from undergraduates, their preparation programs most often parallel the conventional model.

But yet other types of individuals are seeking to become teachers. Some have acquired extensive substitute teaching experience and seek to gain regular faculty positions. Some are building on years of experience as teacher assistants, or work in child care agencies, or involvement in community and church school programs. Some are skilled technicians or accomplished professionals in other fields whose involvement in teaching is limited to a specialized course. And some individuals are those who, for whatever reason, simply elect not to follow the conventional designs.

For these individuals, very unconventional preparation and practice experiences are often their means of becoming teachers. They may begin with intense study in the weeks before the school year begins and then participate in workshops and seminars during the year as they teach. Or they may be "apprenticed" to an experienced teacher for a period of time, after which they are assigned to their own classes. Some are employed on a part-time basis so they can participate in pre/in-service experiences or enroll in courses of study which are designed to enhance their teaching practice. These unconventional preparation programs may be brief, lasting only several weeks, or may span one or more years.

The variety of conventional and unconventional preparation programs may be necessary to serve the needs and interests of the even wider variety of individuals who intend to become teachers. Some have argued that this variety itself may be a strength of the profession and a grace of its members.

The contribution of teacher preparation to becoming a teacher. While the variety of conventional and unconventional approaches to teacher preparation have quite different designs and components, they might be viewed as contributing to becoming a teacher in a similar way, though perhaps with somewhat differing emphases. Consider again the suggested broader reading of becoming a teacher:

the continuous experience of an individual through which an image of self-as-teacher is formed and refined, and during which knowledge, skills and values appropriate to the work of teaching, as it is to be practiced in a particular context, are acquired and used.

Though very important aspects of this development occur before entry into a preparation program and teaching itself, all preparation programs seek to add to the development of prospective teachers in ways congruent with this reading:

1. Preparation programs seek to help the prospective teacher form an image of self-as-teacher which generally might be characterized as "positive," "able," and "professional." More particular images are the goals of some programs: teacher as "decisionmaker," "artist," "advocate," "change agent," and so on. Programs often help particularize the image a prospective teacher forms: an elementary classroom teacher, a resource room teacher, a mathematics teacher, and so on.

Teacher preparation programs add to the experience of becoming a teacher by prompting a review of images of self-as-teacher acquired as a child and student, images that are often inadequately developed and sometimes inappropriate for the actual practice of teaching. Programs offer the opportunity to encounter new images, to "try them on" for fit.

2. Preparation programs seek to help the prospective teacher acquire knowledge, skills, and values appropriate to the work of teaching. Prospective teachers acquire knowledge of the content to be taught, of child and adolescent development, of human learning and behavior, of the structure of the curriculum, of the role of school as an institution in the society, and so on. They learn skills in planning and delivering instruction, in evaluating student performance, in working with colleagues and parents, in assessing one's own teaching. The prospective teachers also acquire values reflective of the recognition of the worth and uniqueness of each student, of the importance of learning in a complex society, of the provision of opportunity for learning to all students, of the need to be a learner even as a teacher.

Teacher preparation programs provide a conceptual base for the organized, systematic study of teaching practice. They assist the prospective teacher in forming a framework, in part using the already acquired knowledge, skills, and values which the individual brings to the preparation experience. Through such a framework, an individual can plan and pursue the acquisition of other knowledge, skills, and values which will make the structure more complete and usable for teaching. Such a structure is necessarily general, and thus it is usable for guiding practice in a variety of teaching contexts. Having such a framework, an individual has the basis for continuing to learn about and practice teaching.

3. Preparation programs seek to provide experiences in particular contexts, through early field experiences, practica, student teaching, and sometimes teaching itself, during which the images being formed and the knowledge, skills, and values being acquired require particular application.

Teacher preparation programs provide opportunities for the prospective teacher to explore images of self-as-teacher and to apply knowledge, skills, and values in particular settings. Such explorations and applications are important means of learning and are also necessary if those acquisitions are to endure in actual practice. Importantly, programs provide guided experience in which explorations and applications can be undertaken with help and encouragement. They provide "safe" experience in which learning about self-as-teacher and teaching can proceed with maximum result and minimum risk for the prospective teacher.

No preparation program seeks all of these ends. And it is evident that no preparation program, whether it be conventional or unconventional, is successful in achieving these ends with every prospective teacher. Preparation programs are limited in scope and effect. Each to its own degree contributes to the becoming a teacher of each individual who participates. What is also evident, however, is that though some of these ends might be achieved without a preparation program, many of the images, much of the knowledge, skills, and values, and some of the particularization of experience would not readily be part of the experience of becoming a teacher for many individuals without the opportunity of participating in preparation programs.

Thus, teacher preparation programs contribute to becoming a teacher in ways that differ from accumulated prior experience and the experience of teaching itself. These contributions might not otherwise be gained. The combination of these contributions of a teacher preparation program to an individual's becoming a teacher results in yet greater outcomes: (a) for the individual, becoming a teacher is not a matter of imitation and reproduction but rather of invention and creation; (b) for the field, the greater outcome is the advancement of teaching.

Induction and Becoming a Teacher

With such outcomes of teacher preparation programs as suggested above, it would seem unnecessary to be greatly concerned about the further development of the individual as a teacher. Well prepared, the new teacher should be able to begin practice and self-direct the further steps in becoming a teacher. Indeed, historically, that is very often what has been assumed: (a) when the preparation program was completed, the support of the individual for learning about teaching was withdrawn; (b) any subsequent learning was informal and optional, or relegated to selected graduate courses or the in-service study days of the employing school district.

The inadequacy of such an assumption is clearly evident. Researchers and practitioners have for decades reported on the difficulty of the first year of teaching. In many reports, "experiences of new teachers" has been synonymous with "problems of new teachers." Kevin Ryan is one of those educators who has focused on the challenge of beginning teachers, documenting their experiences in texts such as *Don't Smile Until Christmas* (1970), and a decade later, *Biting the Apple* (1980); these accounts show the continuing experience of becoming, and the need of new teachers for support in that development. More recent reports such as Robert Bullough's *First-Year Teacher* (1989) extend this tradition. Articles and books document those problems and point to the need new teachers have for support in addressing them.

While some of those reports undoubtedly reflect the historic limits of teacher preparation programs, the difficulties of first-year teaching cannot be attributed to these limits alone. Indeed, even recognizably well prepared new teachers have faced a challenge in their first years of practice. And though many current teacher preparation programs have become more sophisticated in design— drawing on four decades of research on teaching and teacher education, integrating the study of theory with more extensive and more carefully selected field experience, and shaping the experience to the individuals who would be teachers—the need to extend support to new teachers in their first years has not lessened. Though teacher preparation programs contribute in a unique way to the experience of becoming a teacher, other critical steps in that development are taken after preparation in the first years of teaching. Support for new teachers as they continue to become teachers is crucial.

Perhaps this is even more true today than it might have been when the earlier documentation of the difficulties of first-year teachers appeared. The work of teaching has itself become a greater challenge, even for veteran teachers:

1. Teachers face a wider range of children in classrooms—children who differ in intellectual abilities, cultural backgrounds, background experiences, interests, and learning styles.

2. The curricula which classroom teachers are expected to address is more extensive, more varied, and more prescribed.

3. A greater variety of instructional tools are available for use in classrooms, still including paper and pencil media and workbooks, chalkboards, and displays, but also including multiple texts, learning centers, sophisticated audiovisual materials, and computer technologies; while they enrich the instructional process, they also challenge the teacher to incorporate them effectively and appropriately.

4. Teaching itself seems a more complex task: (a) using knowledge in decision making—both the personal and idio-

syncratic knowledge acquired through experience and the more generalizable knowledge derived from research and scholarship which is now informing practice; (b) working with other adults in the provision of services to children and adolescents—teachers, teacher assistants, parent volunteers, and community resource people, among others; (c) balancing the demands of classroom work with the demands and opportunities of increasing professionalism.

5. The complex work of teaching is now placed in societal and professional contexts characterized by greater sensitivity to accountability, generated by the reform movement of the 1980s. Teachers face and feel an increased individual sense of responsibility for the conduct and outcomes of schooling.

If these changes in teaching present challenges to veteran teachers, then perhaps even more so they challenge new teachers. Starting a career in teaching is, for all these reasons perhaps, more demanding than in past years, when already as many as half of each cohort of beginning teachers left the work within the first five years.

The advent of induction programs. Though the difficulties of first-years teachers have long been documented, it is only within the last decade that there has been a groundswell of interest in addressing the needs of beginning teachers. The response to the challenges of beginning a career in teaching are being addressed through rethinking the *transition* from preparation to practice. State agencies, school districts, and colleges and universities are working on their own or collaborating on means of easing that transition through an array of induction programs.

While the term *induction* is not new, the particular meaning that it has now taken on is somewhat different from the meanings it has formerly been given. Whereas induction often referred to the informal, often reactionary, and ritualistic socialization of new teachers, its use now refers to more sophisticated and systematic efforts to initiate, shape, and sustain the first work experiences of prospective career teachers.

In a recent publication of the Association of Teacher Educators, induction is defined as "a transitional period in teacher education, between preservice preparation and continuing professional development, during which assistance may be provided and/or assessment may be applied to beginning teachers" (Huling-Austin, et al. 1989, 3). Induction is acknowledged as a step in becoming a teacher, different from but related to preparation and longer term career development. Importantly, this definition points to a view of induction as active and productive, in contrast with the view once held of it as a passive and often debilitating experience. Like teacher preparation programs, induction has goals and activities organized into programs that seek to add to the experience of becoming a teacher.

Leslie Huling-Austin et al. (1989) lists five common goals of programs designed to assist beginning teachers:

1. To improve teaching performance

2. To increase the retention of promising beginning teachers

3. To promote the personal and the professional well-being of beginning teachers

4. To satisfy mandated requirements related to induction

5. To transmit the culture of the school system (and the teaching profession) to beginning teachers.

Sandra Odell has condensed a somewhat different set of goals from her review of the literature on practice. They present a more comprehensive view of the purposes of induction programs:

1. To provide continuing assistance to reduce the problems known to be common to beginning teachers

2. To support development of the knowledge and the skills needed by beginners to be successful in their initial teaching positions

3. To integrate beginning teachers into the social system of the school, the school district, and the community

4. To provide an opportunity for beginning teachers to analyze and reflect on their teaching with coaching from veteran support teachers

5. To initiate and build a foundation with new teachers for the continued study of teaching

6. To increase the positive attitudes of beginning teachers about teaching

7. To increase the retention of good beginning teachers in the profession (Huling-Austin et al. 1989, 20–21).

In pursuit of goals such as these, induction programs have been planned and implemented which have involved new teachers in a variety of activities. Descriptions of induction programs—their designs and structures—are appearing in professional journals and are being presented at conferences and workshops. Increasingly, reports of the positive impact such programs are having on the experiences of new teachers are appearing in the literature. It would seem that induction programs have been part of the experience of many recent new teachers; it would also seem that in the future, as programs increase in number, this will be the case for many more.

Though the goals and activities and outcomes of induction programs have been widely reported, less attention has been given to relating induction programs conceptually to other experiences in becoming a teacher. Are they repetitive of preparation programs? Do they simply extend preparation into the first year? Are they the first stage of staff development programs? Or are induction programs and other types of programs disassociated? For that matter, given the broader interpretation of "becoming a teacher" that has been suggested here, just how do induction programs contribute in a unique way to this development?

Toward a Theory of Induction

To understand the contribution of induction programs to becoming a teacher, and to relate these programs to other events in the experience, it is useful to have a conceptual understanding of induction itself. Such an understanding should account for the suggested broad interpretation of becoming a teacher, and would therefore necessarily

integrate the broader life experiences and the contributions of preparation and continuing development.

Having a theory of induction with which to work would be helpful on several levels. Like other theories, it would serve to describe, to
explain, and to predict phenomena associated with induction. Having
a "good" theory—one that does these things well—is a useful basis of
planning induction programs, judging their qualities, and reviewing
their effects.

Three Basic Concepts

A theory of induction might usefully begin with a set of three concepts: teacher competence, teacher performance, and teacher effectiveness. These three concepts were discussed by Donald Medley
(1983) and have been used in thinking about teacher evaluation
(Soar, Medley & Coker 1983). Medley drew important distinctions
among the three concepts, which once drawn, become useful for
building the theory. For the present purposes, the three concepts are
discussed particularly as they might be applied to beginning teachers,
though more generally defined they might just as readily apply to experienced teachers.

Teacher *competence* is the body of knowledge, skills, and values
appropriate to the work of teaching, acquired by an individual. It is
the sum of what a new teacher knows, can do, and values doing. Competence is a unique quality of each new teacher.

Competence is acquired in the experiences of being a child and
student, and through participation in a preparation program. A new
teacher's competence may include in-depth knowledge of a particular
topic acquired through courses of study, knowledge of a particular
management strategy acquired through being a student with whom it
was used, or knowledge of a student subculture acquired through
work in summer camp counseling. A new teacher's competence may
include skills such as being able to create a dramatic effect in classroom presentations, or being able to introduce oneself to strangers
and initiate a collegial relationship. A new teacher's competence may

include values such as a commitment to helping all students learn, a desire to maintain some balance between professional and personal time, or a premium on being respected by colleagues.

Teacher competence is transportable. An individual new teacher brings competence from prior experience and study to the work of teaching in any given classroom and school; she will take her competence along when she moves to the next setting.

Teacher *performance* is the expression of the new teacher's competence through the enactment of the tasks of teaching in a particular context. It is the challenge of using what is known, what skills have been acquired, and what values have been formed, in the particular classroom and school in which one is hired to teach. Context bears heavily on performance. That is, a new teacher is not expected to teach "in the abstract" or "in general," but in actual settings.

Performance tasks include classroom-related activities such as planning, delivering instruction, managing the classroom, and evaluating student accomplishment; they require use of the new teacher's competence in serving specific learners, regarding specific content and drawing on established curricula and instructional materials. Outside of the classroom, performance tasks might include forming associations with other teachers and other professionals, working with parents, and participating in the life and culture of the school, district, and community; again, each task requires applications of competence in particular circumstances with particular people.

Importantly, performance is always context bound. Performance is not transportable. That is, the new teacher does not bring prior performances to the setting of his first year of teaching, nor will he take the present performance with him to the next teaching assignment. Rather it is his competence—augmented as it might or will have been by the experience of performance—that accompanies him to each new teaching assignment.

Teacher *effectiveness* is the accomplishment of intended outcomes as a result of performance. Most typically, such outcomes are related to student learning and student behavior. But intended outcomes of performance are also related to out-of-classroom tasks such as becoming part of the faculty, working with parents, and understanding and working with the culture of the school and community.

Like teacher performance, teacher effectiveness is always context bound—expressed in a particular, real setting. Measures and standards of effectiveness vary from context to context. Indicators of student accomplishment in one classroom might not be useful or valued indicators in another. Similarly, indicators of effective work with parents or colleagues in one setting may not be appropriate or used in another. Thus, teacher effectiveness, like performance, is not transportable. The new teacher does not bring her effectiveness with her to the new teaching assignment, but rather it is her competence—augmented as it might have been by prior experiences of effectiveness—that accompanies her.

Four principles

The theory of induction further develops by relating these three concepts to one another through a set of principles:

Teacher competence is the basis of teacher performance. New teachers who have acquired appropriate knowledge, skills, and values have the basis on which they may begin to enact the tasks of teaching in a particular context; persons who have not acquired competence do not have a basis for performance. While it is possible for even incompetent persons to perform as teachers on occasion, sustained performance can be based only on competence.

Teacher performance is the basis of teacher effectiveness. Without the enactment of the tasks of teaching in the particular settings to which they have been assigned, the new teacher's accomplishment of intended outcomes is in doubt. Again, while it is possible that intended outcomes may be reached on occasion without appropriate performance, sustained effectiveness can be expected only from appropriate performance.

Though teacher competence grounds teacher performance, it does not guarantee teacher performance. Thus, new teachers may have appropriate knowledge, skills, and values, but may not know how or may not be able to express them in the particular context in which they are expected to perform.

Though teacher performance grounds teacher effectiveness, it does not guarantee teacher effectiveness. New teachers may enact the tasks of teaching, but the intended outcomes may not be accomplished, or may not be accomplished in terms of local measures and standards.

Consider how these concepts and principles of the emerging theory may describe, explain, and predict the experience of individuals who have prepared for teaching and are about to enter their first year of teaching. The beginning teachers are competent. They have acquired knowledge, skills, and values appropriate to teaching. The new teachers bring their competence to the particular context in which they have been hired to teach. But that competence will require specific interpretation and adaptation in the new contexts. Furthermore, the knowledge, skills, and values that have been acquired and are brought by the new teacher may be ill-formed or inappropriate for use in a given setting. And finally, the new teachers will not likely have acquired all the knowledge, skills, and values needed for teaching in the setting in which they are expected to perform. These conditions do not mean that the new teachers are incompetent. Rather it suggests that their knowledge, skills, and values may need to be interpreted for application, refined, or augmented.

Very often, new teachers have performed well in other settings. They have enacted the tasks of teaching to the satisfaction of their master teachers and supervisors in field experiences and student teaching. In many instances, their effectiveness has been reported in terms of the academic achievement of their students and in terms of their success in becoming part of the faculty and school community. The reviews of their performance and reports of their effectiveness are further evidence of their competence.

This combination of acquired competence, successful performance, and evident effectiveness ought to be the grounds for another important characteristic of new teachers: self-confidence. The new teachers ought to be able to draw on their own sense of being competent, and their histories of performance and effectiveness in approaching their new teaching assignments. This combination of competence, performance, and effectiveness is the best basis and the surest predictor of future success. Being confident of oneself as a beginning teacher—particularly because of one's competence and past performances and effectiveness—is an important grounds for continuing development in the first year of teaching and beyond.[1]

The Contribution of Induction to Becoming a Teacher

A new understanding of induction emerges from the theory. This understanding differs from some popular beliefs about the needs of beginning teachers. Induction is not a process in which the deficits of the preparation program are to be remedied. Nor is induction a means of teaching the neophyte everything that needs to be known for a lifetime of practice in the "real world." Induction is not simply the experience of socialization of the new teacher to the local culture of teaching. And induction should not be the extension of a screening device for the newly hired.

Seen as part of the experience of becoming a teacher, induction might be better understood as follows: *Induction is an effort to assist new teachers in performing—that is, expressing their competence in the particular context to which they have been assigned—toward the end of being effective. Through induction, new teachers continue to form and refine their images of themselves as teachers in terms of their competence, performance, and effectiveness.*

Induction remains a highly individualized experience. Each new teacher brings to it a unique set of qualities which require a unique response. Furthermore, the focus of development is *in* each new teacher. The new teacher necessarily plays an active role in the experience of becoming.

Programs which are planned for the induction of new teachers hope to achieve these ends through the design of mechanisms and activities which hold the promise of adding to each individual's experience of becoming a teacher. Importantly, each new teacher acts as one of the designers of the experience. Using the language of the emerging theory, induction programs (a) assist new teachers as they interpret and adapt their competence for performing in the particular context, toward being effective; (b) provide new teachers the opportunity and means to acquire new competence which they see as needed to perform in that context; and (c) help new teachers convert their present experiences into competence on which to build future practice. Induction programs build on the experience of becoming a teacher already established within the individual, and thus build on what is the basis of the new teacher's self-confidence. The result of an induction program is a competent, performing, and effective teacher, who on these bases is increasingly confident in approaching the work of teaching.

Induction Through Mentoring

The emerging theory of induction describes how induction fits into the experience of becoming a teacher. It suggests that induction comes at a particular time in that development—after a period of preparation and as the new teacher faces the challenge of expressing his competence in the new context in which he is expected to perform and be effective.

The emerging theory does not specify how that assistance is to be provided. Presumably there are a number of alternative means—informal and formal—by which it can be accomplished. Indeed, as programs of induction have been initiated across the country, it is clear that as teacher educators think about this matter, they have designed a variety of mechanisms and activities which they judge to be good means to this end.

One means by which induction support can be provided is through mentoring. Whereas this support mechanism has traditionally been informal and available to only some new teachers as they enter the field, increasingly it is becoming the central feature of formal induction programs. The use of mentoring in formalized programs of induction not only makes the experience of having a mentor available to all new teachers who are to be served, but it also brings a valued dimension to the induction effort that is not part of programs that use other means of addressing matters of competence, performance, and effectiveness. Induction through formal mentoring is increasingly being seen by teacher educators on campus and in the field as the induction program of choice.

The term *mentoring* comes from Homer's classical Greek story, *The Odyssey.* This term suggests older, more experienced persons who assist younger people as they face the challenges of becoming adults. In recent years, recognizing its potential, a number of business, industrial, and professional organizations have adopted mentoring or mentoring-like arrangements for supporting their new employees and colleagues. Reports of the success of such efforts have renewed interest in mentoring in the field of education, including teacher education. Mentoring as a means of educating schoolchildren and adolescents is being explored. Mentoring as means of responding to the long-standing call for support of new teachers is taking hold as a standard in induction practice.

There have been a number of useful analyses of the concept of mentoring as applied to the support of new teachers. Nathalie Gehrke (1988, 44–45) noted particular qualities in a mentor-protege relationship that distinguishes it from other helping roles. She drew on the philosophical work of Martin Buber to suggest that a mentoring relationship is better characterized as an "I-Thou" relationship. Toward such an end, she offered eight points of guidance to those who would promote mentoring.

1. Allow both the mentor and protege to choose each other.

2. Provide time for the relationship to develop.

3. Allow for negotiation of what is to be addressed in the relationship.

4. Assure growing independence and equality for the protege.

5. Acknowledge the uniqueness of both mentor and protege.

6. Accept a reciprocal influence in the relationship.

7. Include a "whole life vision" in the substance of the relationship.

8. Encourage dialogue in the relationship.

Programs which are able to incorporate these points of guidance are more likely to promote relationships that could be termed mentoring relationships.

Eugene Anderson and Anne Lucasse Shannon (1988, 40) offered a definition of mentoring which includes the following attributes:

1. the process of nurturing

2. the act of serving as a role model

3. five functions of the mentor (teaching, sponsoring, encouraging, counseling, and befriending)

4. a focus on professional and/or personal development

5. an ongoing caring relationship.

These attributes, taken together, offer a description of both the mentor's role and the direction the relationship takes.

In the New York State Mentor Teacher-Internship (MTI) Program, the establishment of mentoring relationships between highly regarded experienced teachers and qualified beginning teachers is the chief means to the end of successful induction (Mackey 1989). In a pair of reports on the MTI Program (Mager et al. 1987; Mager & Corwin 1988), on data collected from participating mentor teachers and intern teachers, a very pragmatic view of mentoring was developed. How the mentors and interns were selected, the backgrounds of the participants, and the qualities considered important in matching mentors and interns were described. The initial contacts between mentors and interns, the mentors' first steps, the uses of the released time provided were also detailed. Finally, how the relationships developed, problems encountered in the relationships, the reported impact of the relationships on the interns and mentors, and the prospects for continuing the relationships were summarized.

From these reports and other experiences in the MTI Program, a set of descriptors of mentors and the act of mentoring were condensed and discussed (Mager 1989, 17–19). The descriptors are building on classroom success, having appropriate motives, feeling responsible, dealing with ambiguity, having self-confidence, starting positively, communicating openness to learning, recognizing the importance of being effective, engaging in appropriate activities, focusing on appropriate matters, displaying flexibility, sharing in decisions, being responsive, being available, learning and renewing, trusting and being trustworthy, and feeling rewarded. These descriptors match well with several of the points offered by Gehrke and the attributes offered by Anderson and Shannon. Given that they were derived from the study of the experiences of intern and mentor teachers, they suggest that developing authentic mentoring relationships even in the context of a statewide program is not only possible but occurring.

Mentoring and the Emerging Theory of Induction

Consider how the provision of support through mentoring relates to the experience of becoming a teacher and the emerging theory of induction as discussed above. Already well established are several key points:

1. Becoming a teacher is a continuous experience, unique in form and content to each individual. That uniqueness extends through the preparation program, through the induction experience, and through the teaching career.

2. Competence, performance, and effectiveness are key concepts in understanding the induction experience. New teachers and those who would support them can use these concepts to describe their experience and to plan for induction.

3. Views of one's competence, performance, and effectiveness are woven into the image of self-as-teacher formed by the individual and provide the basis of self-confidence.

4. Context is a crucial factor in the experience of be-coming a teacher, particularly as it relates to the concepts of performance and effectiveness.

5. In becoming a teacher, the individual plays an active role, particularly through the period of preparation and in-duction. Acknowledging the individual's prerogative to do so is fundamental to supporting the experience of becoming.

Given the nature of the experience of becoming a teacher, and given the emerging theory of induction as it is presented here, no ap-proach to providing support and guidance or shaping the experience of new teachers seems as well suited as mentoring. Through a mentor, the unique experience of becoming a teacher that an individual brings to the first year of teaching can be acknowledged and used as the basis of the development at hand. The unique, important image of self-as-teacher can be accepted. Through a mentor, a new teacher has the opportunity to play an active role, negotiating the experience, moving it in directions that are most valued. Through a mentor, a new teacher has access to guidance from a colleague who has successfully faced the challenge of expressing competence, that is, performing and performing effectively, in the particular context in which the new teacher must now do the same. Successes and shortfalls in meeting that challenge can be held in perspective. Appropriate self-confidence can be preserved.

By initiating and sustaining mentoring relationships between be-ginning teachers and their carefully selected veteran colleagues, in-duction programs can "fit with" the unique experience of becoming a teacher, and augment it in a most highly and appropriately person-alized way.

Possibilities, Probabilities, and Induction

It has been the purpose of this chapter to develop an understanding of induction in the broader experience of becoming a teacher. Toward that end, what it is to become a teacher has been reconsidered. The contribution of teacher preparation programs to that development has been explored, and related to the reemergence of interest in support for new teachers. The nature of induction was discussed particularly through the presentation of a theory of induction. This theory can be used to broadly describe, explain, and perhaps predict the experience of first-year teaching; it is also useful to consider in designing induction programs. The chapter ends with the consideration of one form of induction experience, which is increasingly being incorporated in induction programs: mentoring.

Of course, as long as schools are organized for the education of the young, and teachers teach in them, some children and adolescents will begin to become teachers. Perhaps, strangely, even some like Tom Tyker will see that possibility within themselves.

Probably as long as schools are schools and teachers teach, there will be teacher preparation programs—conventional and unconventional—which will seek to shape the experience of individuals becoming teachers. And probably they will do so in different ways and with varying degrees of success.

Probably, as more is expected of schools and teachers, and as more is understood about teaching and learning, the challenges of starting a career in teaching will grow rather than diminish.

Now, for the first time in the history of teaching and schooling, it seems possible that serious, sustained, and widespread attention will be brought to the induction period of becoming a teacher. Through this attention, the experience can be shaped to enhance rather than disrupt that development. But it seems too early to say whether attention to induction is a probability. It seems too early to say whether interest and support for the design and implementation of induction programs will continue, or will give way to other matters of schooling and teaching. That probability will develop only when the efficacy of induction programs is established and widely recognized. It is toward that end that teacher educators, on campuses and in the field, must now work.

Note

1. This theory also helps interpret the experience of veteran teachers who experience difficulty in making transitions from one teaching assignment to another (see Mager et al. 1986). These teachers don't suddenly become incompetent but may need time and assistance in finding how to express their competence in the new setting. Furthermore, the theory may be an alternative interpretation to the phenomenon of teacher burnout: Though the teacher has not changed, the demands of the context in which she or he is expected to perform have changed; thus performance and effectiveness are in jeopardy. For these teachers, augmenting their competence with appropriate knowledge, skills, and values may be the key to becoming effective performers once again.

Bibliography

Anderson, E. M.; and Shannon, A. L. (1988). Toward a conceptualization of mentoring. *Journal of Teacher Education, 39*(1), 38–42.

Applegate, J. H.; Flora, V. R.; and Lasley, T. J. (1980). New teachers seek support. *Educational Leadership, 38*(1), 74–76.

Ball, S. J.; and Goodson, I. F. (1985). *Teachers' lives and careers.* Philadelphia: The Falmer Press.

Berliner, D. C. (1984). The half-full glass: A review of research on teaching. In P. L. Hosford, ed., *Using what we know about teaching.* Alexandria, VA: Association for Supervision and Curriculum Development.

Bey, T. M.; and Holmes, C. T., eds. (1990). *Mentoring: Developing successful new teachers.* Reston, VA: Association of Teacher Educators.

Blackburn, J. (1977, April). The first year teacher: Perceived needs, intervention strategies and results. Paper presented at the American Educational Research Association Annual Meeting, New York. (ERIC Document Reproduction Service, No. ED 135 768).

Bova, B. R.; and Phillips, R. R. (1984). Mentoring as a learning experience for adults. *Journal of Teacher Education, 35*(3), 16–20.

Bower, A. M. (1991). The nature of formalized mentor-intern relationships in a beginning teacher induction program. (Doctoral dissertation, Syracuse University). *Dissertation Abstracts International, 51*(7), 2349A.

Brooks, D. M., ed. (1987). *Teacher induction—A new beginning.* Reston, VA: Association of Teacher Educators.

Bullough, R. V. (1989). *First-year teacher: A case study.* New York: Teachers College Press.

Burke, P.; and Schmidt, W. (1984). Entry year assistance: A promising practice. *Action in Teacher Education, 6*(1–2), 70–74.

Burke, P. J.; Christensen, J. C.; and Fessler, R. (1984). *Teacher career stages: Implications for staff development.* (Fastback No. 214). Bloomington, IN: Phi Delta Kappa Educational Foundation.

Daloz, L. A. (1986). *Effective teaching and mentoring.* San Francisco: Jossey-Bass.

DeBolt, G. P. (1990). Helpful elements in the mentoring of first-year teachers. (Doctoral dissertation, Syracuse University). *Dissertation Abstracts International, 50*(7), 2020A.

Duke, D. L. (1984). *Teaching—The imperiled profession.* Albany, NY: State University of New York Press.

Egan, J. B. (1986). A descriptive study of classroom teachers' mentor-protege roles and relationships. (Doctoral dissertation, Syracuse University). *Dissertation Abstracts International, 47*(5), 1696A.

Flora, V. R. (1979). An exploratory study of teacher development in a confident relationship. (Doctoral dissertation, Ohio State University). *Dissertation Abstracts International, 40*(04), 2010A.

Fuller, F. F.; and Bown, O. (1975). Becoming a teacher. In K. Ryan, ed., *Teacher Education.* The seventy-fourth yearbook of the National Society for the Study of Education, Part 2. Chicago: The University of Chicago Press.

Galvez-Hjornevik, C. (1985). *Mentoring: A review of the literature with a focus on teaching.* Austin: University of Texas, Research and Development Center for Teacher Education. (ERIC Document Reproduction Service, No. ED 262 032).

Gehrke, N. J. (1988). On preserving the essence of mentoring as one form of teacher leadership. *Journal of Teacher Education, 39*(1), 43–45.

Gehrke, N. J.; and Kay, R. S. (1984). The socialization of beginning teachers through mentor-protege relationships. *Journal of Teacher Education, 35*(3), 21–24.

Glassberg, S. (1980, April). A view of the beginning teacher from a developmental perspective. Paper presented at the American Educational Research Association Annual Meeting, Boston.

Haipt, M. (1990, November). A guide for the voyage. *Momentum,* 16–19.

Hall, G. E.; and Loucks, S. (1978). Teacher concerns as a basis for facilitating and personalizing staff development. *Teachers College Record, 80*(1), 36–53.

Hanson, S.; Shulman, J.; and Bird, T. (1985, November). California Mentor Teacher Program Case Study: Implementation in the Orchard Unified School District, 1984–1985. San Francisco: Far West Laboratory for Educational Research and Development.

Harder, M. E. (1990). Teacher satisfaction: Professional needs and basic needs as perceived by mentor teachers. (Doctoral dissertation, Syracuse University). *Dissertation Abstracts International, 51*(1), 25A.

Hitz, R.; and Roper, S. (1986). The teacher's first year: Implications for teacher educators. *Action in Teacher Education, 8*(3), 65–71.

Homer. *The Odyssey.* New York: The New American Library.

Howey, K. R.; and Bents, R. H., eds. (1979). *Toward meeting the needs of the beginning teacher.* Minneapolis: Midwest Teacher Corps Network and University of Minnesota/St. Paul Schools Teacher Corps Project.

Huffman, G.; and Leak, S. (1986). Beginning teachers' perceptions of mentors. *Journal of Teacher Education, 37*(1), 22–25.

Huling-Austin, L. (1986). What can and cannot reasonably be expected from teacher induction programs. *Journal of Teacher Education, 37*(1), 2–5.

Huling-Austin, L.; Barnes, S.; and Smith, J. J. (1985). A research-based staff development program for beginning teachers. (Rep. No. 7201). Austin: University of Texas, Research and Development Center for Teacher Education.

Huling-Austin, L.; Odell, S. J.; Ishler, P.; Kay, R. S.; and Edelfelt, R. A. (1989). *Assisting the beginning teacher.* Reston, VA: Association of Teacher Educators.

James, T. L. (1987, February). Lesson learned: Establishing mentoring roles in two preparation-induction programs. Mentoring as a support system model. Paper presented at the Association of Teacher Educators National Conference.

Krajewski, R. J.; and Shulman, R. B. (1979). *The beginning teacher: A practical guide to problem solving.* Washington: National Education Association.

Lasley, T., ed. (1986). Teacher induction: Programs and research. *Journal of Teacher Education, 37*(1).

Levine, L. M. (1987). Mentoring in the career development of administrators and supervisors in public elementary and secondary schools. (Doctoral dissertation, Rutgers University). *Dissertation Abstracts International, 47*(8), 2829A.

Levinson, D. J.; Darrow, C. N.; Klein, E. B.; Levinson, M. H.; and McKee, B. (1978). *The seasons of a man's life.* New York: Alfred A. Knopf.

Lowney, R. G. (1986). *Mentor teachers: The California model.* (Fastback No. 247). Bloomington, IN: Phi Delta Kappa Educational Foundation.

Mackey, C. C. (1989). The mentor teacher: Rediscovering teacher leadership. *Impact on Instructional Improvement, 22*(3), 20–23.

Mager, G. M. (1989). New teacher induction through mentoring. *Impact on Instructional Improvement, 22*(3), 16–19.

Mager, G. M.; Bower, A.; Corwin, C.; Davis, M.; and DeBolt, G. (1987). *A report to the State Education Department on the New York State mentor teacher-internship program for 1986–1987.* Syracuse: Syracuse University, School of Education. (ERIC Document Reproduction Service, No. ED 303 421).

Mager, G. M.; Cianfarano, S.; and Corwin, C. (1990). *A report to the State Education Department on the New York State mentor teacher-internship program for 1986–1987 and 1987–1988: A follow-up on the experiences of intern teachers.* Syracuse: Syracuse University, School of Education.

Mager, G. M.; Corwin, C. (1988). *A report to the State Education Department on the New York State mentor teacher-internship program for 1987–1988: The mentor-intern relationship.* Syracuse: Syracuse University, School of Education. (ERIC Document Reproduction Service, No. ED 312 234).

Mager, G. M.; and Egan, J. B. (1985, February). From novice to professional: The development of teachers' careers. Paper presented at the Association of Teacher Educators National Conference, Las Vegas.

Mager, G. M.; Myers, B.; Maresca, N.; Rupp, L.; and Armstrong, L. (1986). Changes in teachers' work lives. *The Elementary School Journal, 86*(3), 345–357.

McDonald, F. J. (1980). *Study of induction programs for beginning teachers.* Princeton, NJ: Educational Testing Service. (ERIC Document Reproduction Service, No. ED 257 776).

McNergney, R. F.; and Carrier, C. A. (1981). *Teacher development.* New York: Macmillan.

Medley, D. M. (1983, December). Myths of teacher evaluation. In *Groundwork for the future.* Symposium conducted as part of the fiftieth anniversary celebration of the School of Education, Syracuse University.

Newberry, J. M. (1977, April). The first year of experience: Influences on beginning teachers. Paper presented at the American Educational Research Association Annual Meeting, New York. (ERIC Document Reproduction Service, No. ED 137 299).

Newcombe, E. (1988). *Mentoring programs for new teachers.* Philadelphia: Research for Better Schools.

Newman, K. K. (1978). Middle-aged experienced teachers' perceptions of their career development (Doctoral dissertation, Ohio State University). *Dissertation Abstracts International, 39*(08), 4885A.

————. (1980). Stages in an unstaged occupation. *Educational Leadership, 37*(6), 514–516.

Odell, S. J. (1987). Induction support of new teachers: A functional approach. *Journal of Teacher Education, 37*(1), 26–29.

Phillips-Jones, L. (1983). Establishing a formalized mentoring program. *Training and Development Journal, 37*(2), 38–42.

Ryan, K., ed. (1970). *Don't smile until Christmas.* Chicago: The University of Chicago Press.

————. (1979). Survival is not good enough: Overcoming the problems of beginning teachers. (AFT Quest Paper No. 15). Washington: The American Federation of Teachers.

————. (1986). *The induction of new teachers.* (Fastback No. 237). Bloomington, IN: Phi Delta Kappa Educational Foundation.

Ryan, K.; Applegate, J.; Flora, V. R.; Johnson, J.; Lasley, T.; Mager, G.; and Newman, K. (1979). "My teacher education program? Well...": First-year teachers reflect and react. *Peabody Journal of Education, 56*(4), 267–271.

Ryan, K.; Newman, K.; Mager, G.; Applegate, J.; Lasley, T.; Flora, R.; and Johnston, J. (1980). *Biting the apple: Accounts of first year teachers.* New York: Longman.

Sacks, S. R.; and Brady, P. (1985, April). Who teaches the city's children? A study of New York City first year teachers. Paper presented at the American Educational Research Association Annual Meeting, Chicago.

Shea, J. (1982). The New Florida Beginning Teacher Program. Gainesville, FL: University of Florida. (ERIC Document Reproduction Service, No. ED 230 552).

Sheehy, G. (1974). *Passages: Predictable crises of adult life.* New York: E. P. Dutton.

Shulman, J. (1986). Opportunities of a mentorship: The implementation of the California Mentor Teacher Program. Paper presented at the American Educational Research Association Annual Meeting, San Francisco. (Draft manuscript). San Francisco: Far West Laboratory for Educational Research and Development.

Shulman, J.; Hanson, S.; and King, R. (1985, November). California Mentor Teacher Program Case Study: Implementation in the Waverly Unified School District, 1984–1985. San Francisco: Far West Laboratory for Educational Research and Development.

Smith, D. C., ed. (1983). *Essential knowledge for beginning teachers.* Washington: American Association of Colleges for Teacher Education and ERIC Clearinghouse on Teacher Education.

Soar, R. S.; Medley, D. M.; and Coker, H. (1983). Teacher evaluation: A critique of currently used methods. *Phi Delta Kappan, 65*(4), 239–246.

Tabachnick, B. R.; Zeichner, K. M.; Densmore, K.; Adler, S.; and Egan, K. (1982, March). The impact of the student teaching experience on the development of teacher perspectives. Paper presented at the American Educational Research Association Annual Meeting, New York.

The Toledo Plan: Intern, Intervention, Evaluation. (1985). Toledo, OH: Toledo Federation of Teachers and Toledo Public Schools.

Veenman, S. (1984). Perceived problems of beginning teachers. *Review of Educational Research, 54*(2), 143–178.

Weber, C. E. (1980). Mentoring. *Directors and Boards, 5*(3), 17–24.

What difference does teaching experience make? (1984, Summer). *IRT Communication Quarterly, 7*(1), 3. East Lansing, MI: Michigan State University, Institute for Research on Teaching.

Williams, D. D.; Eiserman, W. D.; and Lynch, P. (1985, April). Understanding problems faced by first year teachers: A naturalistic study. Paper presented at the American Educational Research Association Annual Meeting, Chicago, IL.

Zey, M. G. (1984). *The mentor connection.* Homewood, IL: Dow Jones-Irwin.

2.   Mentoring as Part of Induction

GARY P. DEBOLT

*As noted in chapter 1, mentoring is not a new concept. This chapter will
examine the literature on mentoring in education. In an effort to provide
more background for the reader, it will develop some of the points of mentoring that were introduced in chapter 1.*

The literature on mentoring of first-year teachers is growing. Since
the popularization of the term *mentoring* in the late 1970s, articles
and books have begun to appear which present theories of how mentoring can be conceptualized and how it might be put into practice.
In order to better understand the terms *mentor* and *mentoring* and
how they have been and might be applied to the support of beginning
teachers, this chapter will examine the literature by looking at the
historic background of the term mentor and the mentoring of first-
year teachers.

Historic Background of the Term 'Mentor'

This review of the literature began with the question, "What is a mentor?" The term *mentor* can be traced back to Homer's epic poem, *The
Odyssey.* The original Mentor, a combination of the goddess Athena
and man, was entrusted with the care and guidance of Odysseus' son,
Telemachus. In this great tale, Mentor's complex role was twofold: to
care for Telemachus while guiding the young man to adulthood; and
to help Odysseus fulfill his life's quest by preparing Telemachus to
stand by his father in their fight to regain control of their home in
Ithaca (Daloz 1986). It has been noted that perhaps Mentor's greatest

challenge was "to help Telemachus see the error in his judgment in a way that would allow the young protege to grow in wisdom and not in rebellion" (Clawson 1980, as cited in Galvez-Hjornevik 1986). Mentor served as a role model, guide, facilitator, and supportive protector for Telemachus.

Throughout *The Odyssey,* Mentor helps Telemachus to grow and to learn. Mentor did not work in isolation as he guided Telemachus on his quest for knowledge about his father's fate. When Telemachus ventured out in search of his father, he talked to Odysseus' old comrades and in hearing them talk of the past, he learned and added to his understanding of the adult world. Mentor, through his support and facilitation of the young man's travels, helped Telemachus to experience this learning and to draw meaning and understanding, both of his role in the adult world and of himself as an adult, from his experiences.

Mentor supported and encouraged Telemachus in his search for adulthood; but, he did not attempt to make the younger man the clone of himself nor Odysseus. There was not the expectation that Telemachus would become the equal of his mentor or his father. For example, near the end of *The Odyssey,* Telemachus still was unable to string his father's bow to shoot the arrow through the twelve axeheads (p. 327–328). Nor did Mentor fight Telemachus' battles for him. Mentor (Athena) stood by and watched as Odysseus and Telemachus killed their enemies (p. 345).

In many ways, the task of the original Mentor had been to prepare his friend's son for manhood. This might be viewed as a passing of the torch of leadership to the next generation. Telemachus spoke to his father of the success of his Mentor: "Thou shalt see me, if thou wilt, dear father, in this my mood no whit disgracing thy line, according to thy word" (p. 382). Indeed, Mentor was a transitional aide to adulthood in this famous, ancient Greek story.

Another mentoring relationship can be observed in Dante's *The Divine Comedy.* In this classic poem, the Roman poet Virgil guided Dante in his journey through Hell. As Daloz (1986) noted: "Virgil knows the territory. He is Mentor Supreme, alternately protecting his charge from threat, urging him on, explaining the mysteries, pointing the way, leaving him alone, translating arcane codes, calming marauding beasts, clearing away obstacles, and encouraging—always encouraging" (p. 28). Virgil helps Dante through his journey and when his task is completed he leaves his protege. Thus, this mentor was also a transitional figure who helped his protege to move toward self-knowledge.

For centuries, a mentor was thought of as an older, more experienced person who assisted a younger person (Murray 1908). Roles similar to mentors can be found in at least one non-Western culture. The mythology of the Iroquois of North America contains a vivid example of mentoring. In their "Confederacy Myth," the two great cultural heroes of the Iroquois were involved in what might be described as a mentoring relationship. Deganawidah, the founder of the Iroquois Confederacy, acted as a mentor to Hiawatha. According to the story, Deganawidah helped Hiawatha to reform and to become a good man. Deganawidah did so by serving as a "mirror" in which Hiawatha saw reflected the goodness which existed within himself. This metaphor, of mentor-as-mirror, depicts one man assisting another to realize his own worth and potential. The transformation of Hiawatha from an evil to a good man allowed him to help found the Great Confederacy of the Iroquois. Great societal good came out of this mentoring relationship. Like Mentor, Deganawidah was also a transitional figure who removed himself from the relationship with his protege when his task was accomplished (Wallace 1946).

Recently the term *mentor* has appeared often in the literature on teacher induction and in several other fields of study. This popularity might be attributable, at least in part, to the publication in the 1970s of two books. Both Gail Sheehy's *Passages* (1976) and Daniel J. Levinson's *The Seasons of a Man's Life* (1978) were instrumental in reintroducing the term *mentor* into popular culture. Although Sheehy's work preceded Levinson's in publication, her work was based in part on interviews with Levinson about his work. For this reason, it is useful to examine Levinson's conceptualization of a mentor. In discussing the mentor relationships that he had observed in the lives of adults, Levinson wrote:

> The mentor is ordinarily several years older, a person of greater experience and seniority in the world the young man is entering. No word currently in use is adequate to convey the nature of the relationship we have in mind here. Words such as "counselor" or "guru" suggest the more subtle meanings, but they have other connotations that would be misleading. The term "mentor" is generally used in a much narrower sense, to mean teacher, adviser or sponsor. As we use the term, it means all these things, and more. (p. 97).

Indeed, the term *mentor* is portrayed as a complex concept.

Since these important books were published, many articles and some books have asserted the value, importance, and even necessity of mentors (Speizer 1981). More recently the term *mentor* has come loosely to mean: teacher, coach, trainer, role model, protector, sponsor, leader, or promoter (Galvez-Hjornevik 1986). Mentors can be found in the training and development of nurses, psychologists, sociologists, scientists, and teachers (Gray & Gray 1985). Although mentoring is a much discussed and often used term, there is evidence that it is little understood and vaguely defined. There exists no commonly accepted meaning of the term (Speizer 1981).

Mentoring of First-Year Teachers

Several state or local educational agencies have attempted to improve their preparation of beginning teachers. Some have experimented with specific programs to prepare preservice and in-service teachers for pedagogical decision making. One such program is the University of Virginia's Beginning Teacher Assistance Program (McNergney, Lloyd, Mintz, & Moore 1988). Others have adopted a five-year program to prepare preservice teachers through a carefully structured program which uses cooperating teachers to guide and support the student teachers through that important, developmental experience. The University of New Hampshire operates such a program (Corcoran & Andrew 1988).

Other state or local educational agencies have adopted some form of support, which they have variously called "mentoring," as part of their local or statewide induction programs (California; Toledo, Ohio; North Carolina; New York). A common characteristic among these programs is their vague and often unique definitions of the terms *mentor* and *mentoring* (Anderson & Shannon 1988, Thies-Sprinthall 1986, Gray & Gray 1985). Anderson and Shannon (1988) note that few articles have presented a clear image of mentoring. Further, most reports of mentoring do not provide a conceptual framework for mentoring.

In their article, "Synthesis of Research on Mentoring Beginning Teachers," William A. Gray and Marilynne M. Gray (1985) concluded, "If formalized mentoring is conceptualized and implemented in accord with the Helping Relationship model, it can meet the specific needs of beginning teachers and provide increased professional satisfaction to mentors" (p. 42). Gray and Gray reached this conclusion in spite of the fact that they had to infer much of this potential effect since, as they noted, "most studies of mentoring have been done in the business field" (p. 37) and most often investigated informal mentor-protege (intern) relationships. Many of these studies investigated relationships that had existed several years in the past.

Studies of Informal Mentoring Among Teachers

One example of a study which examined past experiences was N. J. Gehrke and R. S. Kay's 1984 study in which they surveyed teachers to discover if they had known a person who had "helped, guided, or sponsored them" (p. 21) in their lives as teachers. Many of the respondents indicated that they had experienced some form of mentoring relationships at the beginning of their careers. The results of the study indicated that this group of teachers had experienced informal, spontaneous relationships. The researchers found that mentors were genuinely interested in their proteges, helpful, caring, willing to take time, dedicated, friendly, outgoing, patient, influential, and served as professional models.

James B. Egan interviewed thirteen teachers about their recollections of mentors at the beginnings of their teaching careers. He also interviewed six of the mentors identified by teachers. From his study of these classroom teachers' informal mentor-protege roles and relationships, Egan (1985) derived the following definition of mentoring:

> The mentoring of teachers is an empowering process characterized by availability and approachability on the part of an experienced educator, and receptivity by the neophyte. Through this process a beginning teacher receives technical assistance, career advice, and psychological support from an experienced person. This assistance and support is transmitted through observations, ongoing discussions, questionings, and planning together in an adult learning mode. During this process, the experienced educator acts as a role model, teacher, and counselor to the beginner. The influence of the experienced person is pervasive and enduring, while still honoring the autonomy of the neophyte teacher. (p. 197)

Egan's definition serves as a good summation of the positive aspects of the mentor-intern relationship which have been observed in informal mentoring among teachers.

Formalized Mentoring Among Teachers

Cleta Galvez-Hjornevik has also examined the material in this field of study. In her article, "Mentoring Among Teachers: A Review of the Literature" (1986), she stated, "Few studies have been published that focus specifically on teacher-teacher relationships and the phenomenon of mentoring in elementary and secondary schools" (p. 6). The four studies that she noted were investigations of programs for induction which have been reported by Krupp (1984); Little, Galagaran, and O'Neil (1984); Huling-Austin, Barnes, and Smith (1985); and Showers (1984).

Judy Krupp (cited in Galvez-Hjornevik 1986) reported the positive effects of a series of workshops to encourage the development of mentoring relationships in schools in Connecticut. Little, Galagaran, and O'Neil (cited in Galvez-Hjornevik 1986) detailed the "face-to-face" work between teachers and stressed the collegial nature of the relationships. The Model Teacher Induction Project (MTIP) conducted by researchers at The University of Texas at Austin was reported by Huling-Austin, Barnes, and Smith (cited in Galvez-Hjornevik 1986). The results of this study of six first-year teachers suggested the positive benefits of a support teacher as a part of an induction program.

Bruce Joyce and Beverly Showers (1982) have advanced coaching, a term which they use in much the same way others use mentoring, as one way of helping teachers to acquire skills and strategies. Further research in this area has led Showers to argue that one-session workshops or one-day conferences are insufficient to cause a real change in the behavior of teachers. Joyce and Showers have proposed that if programs are to have an effect on the actual teaching behavior of beginning teachers, then they must provide meaningful support to the new teacher throughout the induction period (Joyce & Showers 1982). This line of thought was supported by later work (Showers 1984).

The work of Gerald M. Mager (1988, February; 1988, April; 1988, August; and chapter 1) continued the extensive description of the ongoing effort in New York State to programmatically use mentors in the support of first-year teachers. This large-scale study has chronicled the conceptualization and implementation of mentoring in varied, often unique, contexts. Mager's work has called for further investigation of mentoring in order to better understand the concept and its extended applications in education.

Galvez-Hjornevik further examined the literature of mentoring in other fields and concluded by suggesting, "The vital role allocated the 'mentor teacher' in the induction process necessitates a greater understanding of the potential for this association and its subsequent impact on the education of beginning teachers in our elementary and secondary schools" (p. 10). There is a need to better understand what mentoring is and how it can be enhanced in schools.

The article, "Toward a Conceptualization of Mentoring," by Eugene M. Anderson and Ann L. Shannon (1988) was a seminal piece in the literature on mentoring. The authors argued that recent views of mentoring are inadequate because various definitions (Phillips-Jones 1983, Alleman 1986, Levinson et al. 1978, Zey 1984, and Daloz 1986) fail to specify whether mentoring involves a set of functions that are conjunctively (must all be used together) or disjunctively (may be used individually) joined. Anderson and Shannon proceed to propose an updated concept of mentoring. The essential attributes of Anderson's and Shannon's definition of mentoring are (a) the process of nurturing, (b) the act of serving as a role model, (c) the five mentoring functions (teaching, sponsoring, encouraging, counseling, and befriending), (d) the focus on professional and/or personal development, and (e) the ongoing caring relationship (Anderson & Shannon 1988).

Programmatic Applications of Mentoring

As the literature on mentoring continues to grow, a variety of interpretations and programs of implementation have appeared. In California, mentor teachers have been supported in their efforts to help beginning teachers. Mentors have been encouraged to continue their efforts and to enhance the professionalism of teaching by emphasizing the collegial nature of mentoring and peer-coaching (Shulman 1988).

Joan Ann Ruskus (1988) conducted a study entitled, "A Multi-Site Evaluation of the California Mentor Teacher Program." Her study integrated quantitative and qualitative methods to examine four research propositions, two of which dealt with issues regarding the mentor program and variations in its implementations in five different school districts. The results of the study, which surveyed forty-two mentors, supported the conclusion that the mentor program functioned as an effective incentive for increasing the satisfaction of mentors through intrinsic rewards; however, the program was not an effective retention incentive for mentors (Ruskus 1988, 1–2).

In Connecticut, mentor teachers have been integrated into the Beginning Educator Support and Training Program (BEST). Connecticut provides formal training to prepare mentor teachers to perform their duties. The mentor, with the building administrator, acclimates, supports, and helps the beginning teacher to develop the skills outlined in the Connecticut teaching competencies (Tirozzi 1988).

Pam Littleton and Mark Littleton (1988) have reported the efforts of teacher educators in Texas who have worked to assist beginning teachers in the Beginning Teacher Effectiveness Training (BTET). Beginning teachers are assigned a mentor from a pool of experienced teachers at Level II or Level III of the Texas Career Ladder. Matches are based on gender and subject area. Here, the mentor is thought of as a "guide, friend, and host." The intensity of the mentor's role declines as the novice gains experience and confidence.

Many articles report the implementation of particular conceptualizations of mentoring in education. The list begins to appear as a litany of mentor programs and authors: Franklin County, Ohio (Zimpher 1988, Howey 1988); Virginia (McNergney et al. 1988); New Hampshire (Corcoran & Andrew 1988); North Carolina (Thies-Sprinthall 1986, 1987; and Huffman & Leak 1986); Wisconsin (Varah et al. 1986, Varah 1988, and McKenna 1988); and New York (Mager 1986; Mager et al. 1987; Mager et al. 1988; Mager 1988; Mager 1988; Halkett 1988; Bohler 1988; Wolfe & Stupiansky 1988; O'Brien, Kaufman, Newman & Sole 1988; Smith & Gamble 1988; and Sacks & Wilcox 1988). As a group, they provide valuable insight into the variety of ways that mentoring has been implemented in schools.

The work of Gray and Gray, previously cited, is revealing because it outlined the transitional nature of the literature in the mentoring of beginning teachers. It, as a field of study, is in transition from adaptation of a concept from other fields such as business to application of this concept of mentoring to the induction of new teachers.

Educational journals have devoted entire thematic issues to mentoring (e.g., *Theory Into Practice, 27*[3]). The *Handbook of Research on Teacher Education* (1990), edited by W. Robert Houston, includes a chapter entitled, "Teacher Induction Programs and Internships" by

Leslie Huling-Austin. This chapter reviews studies of induction programs. Huling-Austin concludes by noting the "extensive interest across the nation in teacher induction programs and internships." She further states that a key question in this field of study is "What induction practices work best under what conditions?" This is one of the questions this work addresses.

Judith H. Shulman and Joel A. Colbert have published two useful works entitled, *The Mentor Teacher Casebook* (1987) and *The Intern Teacher Casebook* (1988). These books apply to the California Model of mentoring of new teachers. The works by Shulman and Colbert are part of a larger effort to document "close-to-the-Classroom Casebooks" to record and preserve the experiences of teachers. They include vignettes of mentors' reflections upon their work. These cases are representative of a larger class of experiences (Shulman & Colbert 1987).

In 1989, the National Education Association published *Teacher Induction,* edited by Judy Reinhartz. This volume examines many aspects of the teacher induction process. It includes a synthesis of the research on induction programs, research reports, and a helpful annotated bibliography. Sandra J. Odell provided a detailed analysis of the use of mentoring beginning teachers in *Mentor Teacher Programs* (1990). *Mentoring: Developing Successful New Teachers* (1990), edited by Teresa M. Bey and C. Thomas Holmes, has been published as a monogram by the Association of Teacher Educators. The work resulted from the efforts of The ATE Commission on the Roles and Preparation of Mentor Teachers. It examines the topic of mentoring and its existing knowledge base. It is a useful work.

Although educators have applied a variety of understanding and forms of mentoring, there are some common characteristics of the concept. In most cases, the mentor is seen as helpful; a teacher, a guide, and a coach. The mentor's purpose is to help the new teacher through the experiences and learning of the first year or more of teaching. We need to understand more about the nurturing aspects of this role and the relationship that develops between mentor and new teacher.

Teachers who have already experienced this transitional role can be very helpful in more clearly defining mentoring. We hope to better understand this process through their experience and reflection.

As educators work to more clearly understand mentoring, its required attributes and its activities, we can benefit from an examination of successful programs. The next section of this book will report five school-based collaborative projects which have used mentoring within the context of teacher induction. Each program is unique and offers analysis from its specific set of contexts.

References

Alleman, E. (1986). Measuring mentoring-frequency quality impact. In W. A. Gray and M. M Gray, eds., *Mentoring: Aid to excellence in career development, business and the professions.* British Columbia: The Xerox Reproduction Centre.

Anderson, E.; and Shannon, A. (1988). Toward a conceptualization of mentoring. *Journal of Teacher Education, 39*(1), 38–42.

Bey, T.; and Holmes, C. (1990). *Mentoring: Developing successful new teachers.* Reston, VA: Association of Teacher Educators.

Bohler, C. (1988). *Handbook for mentor/internship program: Jefferson-Lewis-Hamilton-Herkimer-Oneida BOCES.* Unpublished manuscript.

Clawson, J. (1980). Mentoring in managerial careers. In C. B. Derr, ed., *Work, family, and the career.* New York: Proeger.

Corcoran, E.; and Andrew, M. (1988). A full year internship: An example of school-university collaboration. *Journal of Teacher Education, 39*(3), 17–22.

Daloz, L. (1986). *Effective teaching and mentoring.* San Francisco: Jossey-Bass.

Dante, A. (1961). *The Divine Comedy.* (J. D. Sinclair, trans.) New York: Oxford University.

Egan, J. (1985). *A descriptive study of classroom teachers' mentor-protege roles and relationships.* Unpublished doctoral dissertation, Syracuse University, Syracuse, NY.

Galvez-Hjornevik, C. (1986). Mentoring among teachers: A review of the literature. *Journal of Teacher Education, 37*(1), 6–11.

Gehrke, N.; and Kay, R. (1984). The socialization of beginning teachers through mentor-protege relationships. *Journal of Teacher Education, 35*(3).

Gray, W.; and Gray, M. (1985). Synthesis of research on mentoring beginning teachers. *Educational Leadership, 43*(3), 37–43.

Halkett, K. (1988). *Peer assistance and review program 1986/87 local evaluation report.* Rochester, NY: Unpublished manuscript.

Houston, W. R. (1990). *Handbook of research on teacher education.* New York: Macmillan.

Howey, K. (1988). Mentor-teachers as inquiring professionals. *Theory into Practice, 27*(3), 209–213.

Huffman, G.; and Leak, S. (1986). Beginning teachers' perceptions of mentors. *Journal of Teacher Education, 37*(1), 22–25.

Joyce, B.; and Showers, B. (1982, October). The coaching of teaching. *Educational Leadership,* 4–8.

Levinson, D.; Darrow, C.; Klein, E.; Levinson, M.; and McKee, B. (1978). *Seasons of a man's life.* New York: Knopf.

Littleton, P.; and Littleton, M. (1988, September). Induction programs for beginning teachers. *The Clearing House,* 36–38.

Mager, G. (1986). *Support for first-year teachers: New York State's mentor teacher-internship program.* Unpublished manuscript.

———. (1988, April). *New teacher induction through mentoring.* Syracuse, NY. Unpublished manuscript.

———. (1988, August). *A report to the State Education Department on the New York State mentor teacher-internship program for 1987–1988: The analysis of costs.* Syracuse, NY. Unpublished manuscript.

Mager, G.; Bower, A.; Corwin, C.; Davis, M.; and DeBolt, G. (1987). *A report to the State Education Department on the New York State mentor teacher-internship program for 1986–1987.* Unpublished manuscript.

Mager, G.; Corwin, C.; DeBolt, G.; and Harder, M. (1988, February). New York State's mentor teacher-internship program. Paper presented at the meeting of the Association of Teacher Educators, San Diego, CA.

McKenna, G. F. (1988). *Analysis of the benefits of being a mentor in a formal induction program.* Unpublished dissertation: Loyola University of Chicago.

McNergney, R., Lloyd, J.; Mintz, S.; and Moore, J. (1988). Training for pedagogical decision making. *Journal of Teacher Education*, 39(5), 37–43.

Murray, A. H., ed. (1908). A new English dictionary. In E. Anderson and A. Shannon, eds., *Journal of Teacher Education: Sec. 1, Vol. 39. Toward a conceptualization of mentoring*. Oxford: Clarendon.

O'Brien, C.; Kaufman, J.; Newman, D.; and Sole, K. (1988). Mentoring early year teachers: A case study of one school district. Paper presented at the annual meeting of the American Educational Research Association. New Orleans, LA.

Odell, S. J. (1990). *Mentor teacher programs*. Washington, DC: National Education Association.

The Odyssey of Homer. (1950). (S. H. Butcher and A. Lang, trans.) New York: The Modern Library.

Phillips-Jones, L. (1983, February). Establishing a formalized mentoring program. *Training and Development Journal*, 38–42.

Reinhartz, J., ed. (1989). *Teacher induction*. Washington, DC: National Education Association.

Ruskus, J. A. (1988). A multi-site evaluation of the California mentor teacher program. Paper presented at the annual meeting of American Educational Research Association, New Orleans, LA.

Sacks, S.; and Wilcox, K. (1988). *Training retired teachers for the transition to mentoring*. Paper presented at the annual meeting of the American Educational Research Association, New Orleans, LA.

Sheehy, G. (1976). *Passages: Predictable crises of adult life*. New York: Bantam Books.

Showers, B. (1984). Peer coaching and its effects on transfer of training. Paper presented at the annual meeting of the American Educational Research Association, New Orleans, LA.

Shulman, J. (1988, January). Look to a colleague: For inspiration, for insight, for guidance. *Instructor*, 32–34.

Shulman, J.; and Colbert, J. (1987). *The mentor teacher casebook*. San Francisco, CA: Far West Laboratory.

————. (1988). *The intern teacher casebook*. San Francisco, CA: Far West Laboratory.

Smith, A.; and Gamble, M. (1988). A collaborative mentoring model for support of first year teachers. Paper presented at the spring conference of the Confederated Organizations for Teacher Education, Syracuse, NY.

Speizer, J. (1981). Role models, mentors and sponsors: The elusive concepts. *Signs,* 6(4), 692–712.

Thies-Sprinthall, L. (1986). A collaborative approach for mentor training: A working model. *Journal of Teacher Education,* 37(6), 13–20.

Thies-Sprinthall, L.; and Sprinthall, N. (1987). Experienced teachers: Agents for revitalization and renewal as mentors and teacher educators. *Journal of Teacher Education,* 38(1), 65–79.

Tirozzi, G. (1988, April). Architecturing a comprehensive reform of teaching: The Connecticut perspective. Paper presented at the annual meeting of the American Educational Research Association, New Orleans, LA.

Varah, L. (1988, February). The University of Wisconsin-Whitewater teacher induction program. Paper presented at the annual meeting of the Association of Teacher Educators, San Diego, CA.

Varah, L.; Theune, W.; and Parker, L. (1986). Beginning teachers: Sink or swim. *Journal of Teacher Education,* 37(1), 30–34.

Wallace, P. A. (1946). *The white roots of peace.* Port Washington, KY: Kennikat.

Wolfe, M.; and Stupiansky, N. (1988, February). Rural-based mentor/intern project: First year outcomes and the future. Paper presented at the annual meeting of the Association of Teacher Educators, San Diego, CA.

Zey, M. (1984). *The mentor connection.* Homewood, IL: Dow Jones-Irving.

Zimpher, N. (1988). A design for the professional development of teacher leaders. *Journal of Teacher Education,* 39(1), 53–60.

Part II

School-Based Collaborative Programs

This section includes five descriptive reports of the programmatic use of mentoring in induction of new teachers. The reports represent some of the great variety of mentoring programs in use today. Each chapter, like the program it describes, is unique and offers a distinctive flavor in both design and implementation. You, the reader are encouraged to appreciate the distinctly different nature of each program as you look for the similarities of the cases, both to each other and to your particular set of questions or contexts.

3. Collaborative Teacher Induction

SANDRA J. ODELL
DOUGLAS P. FERRARO

In this chapter, Odell and Ferraro describe a successful collaborative men-toring project in New Mexico that involves the Albuquerque Public Schools and the University of New Mexico. The authors provide an overview of the program and its theoretical foundation. The goals, roles of participants, and program funding are explained. The chapter concludes with a report of lessons learned from experience and promising outcomes and benefits of such a program.

Within the teacher education literature a number of different terms have been used to characterize programs of support for teachers who are entering the teaching profession. Such terms have included: (a) beginning teacher assistance programs, (b) clinical support programs, (c) teacher induction programs, and (d) mentor teacher programs. While these different terms sometimes reflect important nuances among programs, more often than not they simply reflect the current zeitgeist in teacher education. Thus, while in the early 1980s the more frequently used term was *teacher induction program,* the contemporary trend is to use the term *mentor teacher program* (Odell 1990a).

Whatever the phraseology used, the object of supportive begin-ning teacher programs is to assist beginning teachers in their pro-fessional growth and to ease their transition from student teacher to full-time instructional leader in the classroom.

What follows herein is a description of a teacher induction pro-gram that involves a school district and a university working together in order to provide beginning teachers with systematic support dur-ing their first year of teaching. Included in this description are the

---

*This chapter appears in part and is an expanded version of: Odell, S. (1990c). Teacher induction: A program that works. *Journal of Staff Development,* 11(4), 12–16.

program's rationale and goals as well as specific information about the components and funding associated with the teacher induction program. Information is also provided about some of the lessons that have been learned and some of the promising outcomes that have been observed during six years of implementing a successful collaborative school district/university program of support for beginning teachers.[1]

Program Overview

The Albuquerque Public Schools/University of New Mexico (APS/ UNM) Teacher Induction Program was established in 1984. It involves a large public school system (eighty-five thousand students) and a university-based college of education that collaborates in offering structured induction support to all entry-level elementary classroom teachers in the school district. The program is directed by a full-time university faculty member who coordinates the communication and decision making between the school system and the university as they relate to teacher induction. When the program was initially conceived, the teacher induction program director, public school personnel, and the university's director of teacher education met weekly in order to collaborate in planning the program's rationale, goals, participants, and funding.

Program Rationale

The rationale for the establishment of the APS/UNM Teacher Induction Program was derived from theories of teacher development, which generally suggest that becoming a fully competent teacher is a lifelong process, and the reality of beginning teaching, which is widely regarded as perilous. Thus, the program rationale was derived from both the theory and practice of beginning teaching. A fuller explication of these two bases for establishing collaborative teacher induction program follows.

Stages of Teacher Development

Teacher development theories generally pertain to the cognitive development of the teacher, teacher concerns, and expertise in teaching. Each of these theoretical perspectives includes a series of developmental stages through which beginning teachers are thought to progress before emerging as truly competent instructional leaders. Hypothetically, well-designed teacher induction interventions would first establish the beginning teacher's current stage of teacher development and then serve to facilitate the beginning teacher's further development toward stages of higher teaching competency (Odell 1987a).

Cognitive development theory postulates that there is a progression in the beginning teacher's stage of conceptual development from simplistic and concrete thinking to analytic and flexible thinking. Teachers at higher stages of development presumably teach so as to produce students who evince higher levels of thinking, self-exploration, and independence. Glassberg (1979) highlighted the importance of cognitive development theory for supporting beginning teachers in teacher induction programs as follows:

> Studies suggest that higher stage teachers tend to be adaptive in teaching style, flexible, tolerant and able to employ a wide range of teaching models. These findings provide further evidence to support the claim that an intervention designed to promote ego, morale, and conceptual development of the beginning teacher will ultimately enhance the teacher's effectiveness in the classroom (p. 125).

Stages of teacher concerns theory recognizes that the concerns of beginning teachers are uniquely different from those of experienced teachers. It postulates that teaching efficacy is enhanced when teachers progress through qualitatively different stages of teacher concerns (Fuller 1969, Glassberg 1979, Katz 1972). Beginning teachers are most concerned about just surviving from day to day. It is not atypical for the first-year teacher to ask, "Does it get better?" or "Will I make it to the end of the week?" or "How do I do a good job and still have a life outside of teaching?" (Odell, Loughlin and Ferraro 1987). Scheduling and organizing the day, functioning within the school system, and classroom discipline are other important beginning teacher concerns (Veenman 1984).

In contrast, experienced teachers are characterized by concerns more directly related to the efficacy of their teaching. They express concerns about the impact that their instruction has on students, about collaborating with other professionals, and about teaching as a profession. From this perspective, a teacher induction program should work toward relieving the negative concerns of beginning teachers and guiding beginning teachers toward concerns that will potentiate rather than inhibit excellent teaching.

Berliner (1986, 1988) addressed the topic of expertise in teaching by postulating that there are five stages in the journey from being a novice teacher to arriving as an expert teacher. These stages are characterized by differences in the ways that teachers interpret happenings in their classrooms. A novice teacher has no past experiences on which to rely in interpreting classroom phenomena. Expert teachers, on the other hand, can more readily predict classroom events since their past experiences provide a frame of references from which to distinguish the typical from the atypical and to pick out what is important from what is not. Within this theory teacher induction support interventions can facilitate the development of a knowledge base in the beginning teacher by reframing their novice experiences from a more expert perspective.

Taken together, theories of teacher development suggest that beginning teachers think quite simplistically and rather noncreatively as they exhibit survival concerns and try to make sense of classroom events. Veteran, expert teachers, on the other hand, think more flexibly as they concern themselves about impacting students from the perspective of their past experiences.

A collaborative teacher induction program is obviously challenged first to understand and accept the initial level of development for beginning teachers, and then to guide beginning teachers to achieve more sophisticated stages of concern and cognitive development. The APS/UNM Teacher Induction Program has accepted the further challenge of fostering the social and emotional development of beginning teachers so as to insulate them from the reality of beginning teaching, which represents the second main rationale for establishing the program.

Reality of Beginning Teaching

Often the new teacher is shocked by the reality of beginning teaching and needs to be socialized into the culture of the school (Lortie 1975). This is because, by its very nature, beginning teaching is a precipitous and perilous enterprise. From the outset beginning teachers are given the same responsibilities as are veteran teachers. No matter how excellent the new teacher's preservice training may have been, no training simulation accurately duplicates the reality of full-time teaching. For example, ultimate classroom responsibilities no longer rest with the cooperating teachers as they did in student teaching. Suddenly, the enormity of the job hits the beginning teacher; a phenomenon that has been termed "reality shock" (Veenman 1984). Indicators of reality shock include complaining about the teaching work load, changing one's teaching in a manner that is contrary to one's beliefs about teaching, manifesting changes in attitudes and personality, and even suddenly leaving the teaching profession altogether (Gray & Gray 1985).

Consider further the anxieties that beginning teachers must face when they are given the most difficult teaching assignments because teachers with seniority are allowed to choose the more desirable assignments (Adams 1982). Having to work with students of low ability or disruptive students, having many different class preparations, having to move from classroom to classroom to teach, and having responsibility for extracurricular activities no doubt compound the stresses experienced by many beginning teachers (Adams 1982, Huling-Austin 1987). Worse still, in the past as many as 12 percent of all newly hired teachers in the United States were not certified in the fields in which they were assigned to teach (Roth 1986).

As if adjustment to their professional teaching roles is not difficult enough, beginning teachers also face a variety of personal concerns (Veenman 1984). They may be criticized for their ideas about teaching, which some veteran teachers consider as too naive or idealistic. Resultant feelings of isolation and inadequacy may be compounded by impatient family members and nonteaching friends who question unbelievably why teaching takes so much time outside of the classroom. Further, some beginning teachers enter a world of adult financial and nonstudent responsibilities that are in stark contrast to the university student life from which they came (Ryan 1986).

Beginning teachers encountering these realities may experience a collapse of the ideals they formed about teaching during teacher training. Cogan (1975) observed that part of what occurs in difficult learning situations is a regression to safer and more familiar behaviors. Research has shown that more than half of beginning teachers change from a student centered teaching approach to an authoritarian way of teaching, and that over 90 percent of beginning teachers make concessions in using a democratic style of teaching because of the difficulties that surface in the classroom (Veenman 1984).

It is not too extreme to conclude that if the realities of beginning teaching are not dealt with constructively, and if beginning teachers are not appropriately supported and encouraged when they are most vulnerable, there will exist the risk of having beginning teachers revert to less effective teaching methodologies (Huling-Austin 1990).

Program Goals

The goals for the APS/UNM Teacher Induction Program were derived directly from the program rationale. From teacher development theory was derived the program goal of guiding the professional development of beginning teachers. From the perilous reality of beginning teaching was derived the program goal of addressing the unique concerns of beginning teachers. These two primary goals are specified below along with two related goals that pertain to other aspects of the program.

√ *Goal one.* To provide beginning teachers with guidance from an excellent veteran teacher in order to facilitate the beginning teacher's professional development.

Two subsidiary goals for achieving beginning teacher development have been earlier described by Odell (1989a). These subsidiary goals are to provide an opportunity for beginning teachers to analyze and reflect on their teaching through coaching, and to build a foundation with beginning teachers so that they become self-reliant in their teaching.

√ *Goal two.* To provide beginning teachers with assistance, support, and information from an excellent veteran teacher in order to decrease the perilous nature of beginning teaching.

Concerns of beginning teachers can be reduced if beginning teachers are integrated into the social fabric and cultural norms of the school and surrounding community. This is accomplished, in part, when they are given information about school district policies and procedures. Specifically put, the lives of beginning teachers are more free of concerns if they know how to arrange for substitute teachers, have positive attitudes toward their colleagues, and sense that they belong in school. Importantly, providing emotional support, positive feedback, patience, and understanding to beginning teachers helps them to reduce the noninstructional concerns that they inevitably have (Brooks 1986).

Goals three and four of the APS/UNM Teacher Induction Program fall somewhat outside of the primary focus on beginning teaching. Rather, they are directed specifically at the veteran teachers who work with the beginning teachers and on the institutions that are involved in the teacher induction program.

Goal three. To provide excellent veteran teachers professional development beyond classroom teaching.

Few opportunities exist for veteran teachers to pursue university course work and professional development opportunities during the school day. This is accomplished in the APS/UNM Teacher Induction

Program by releasing veteran teachers from their teaching responsibilities in order to support beginning teachers and to study teaching in a unique professional context.

Goal four. To create significant collaboration between a public school system and an institution of higher education in the induction of beginning teachers.

Historically institutions of higher education have been involved directly in training teachers at the preservice level. They may have been involved further with experienced teachers through in-service efforts or in providing graduate course work. However, colleges and universities typically have not been involved in the induction of teachers, that is, during the teacher's initial year of teaching. The APS/UNM Program extends the university's involvement to the induction year by providing a faculty member to direct the induction program and to offer course work directly aimed at the preparation of veteran teachers who assist beginning teachers. The university also provides induction courses for beginning teachers.

Program Participants

There are four integral personnel components to the APS/UNM Teacher Induction Program. They include graduate interns, beginning teachers, clinical support teachers, and the program director. All teaching personnel are jointly selected for their roles by the school district and university.

Graduate intern component. Fourteen fully certified university interns work as beginning elementary teachers while also pursuing a master's degree in teaching. The intern assumes yearlong responsibility for an elementary classroom just as would any other beginning teacher. In return, the graduate intern receives a university stipend equal to 60 percent of a beginning teacher's salary, tuition waivers, and credit for their teaching toward a master's degree, which is completed during two summers plus an academic year. Figure 3.1 presents

Figure 3.1
GRADUATE INTERN PROGRAM OF STUDIES
MASTER OF ARTS IN ELEMENTARY EDUCATION
(Emphasis: Teaching)
Minimum: 32 Semester Credit Hours

Required Courses:	Credit Hours
Process of Teaching and Learning	3
Advanced Field Experience	6
Advanced Instructional Strategies	3
Topics/Classroom Practice	2
Curriculum (Early Childhood, Elementary, or Bilingual)	3
Research Applications to Education	3
Education Across Cultures in the Southwest	3
Program Synthesis Seminar	3
Supporting Area: A minimum of six additional hours chosen from the categories of development, cross-cultural studies, language studies, or technology	6

the complete master's degree program of studies for graduate interns.

Graduate interns have a unique opportunity to combine theoretical course work with the practice of teaching while receiving the same induction support as do all the other beginning teachers in the school district. In addition, graduate interns work as a cohort group offering one another support as they progress through their initial teaching year. The school district also gives the graduate interns teaching credit for their graduate intern year on the salary schedule. Thus, following their graduate intern year, graduate interns progress to step two on the experience index, and to a master's degree on the education index, of the school district's salary schedule. In point of fact, graduate interns recover their first-year reduction in salary (as compared to the other beginning teachers) in about three years when the benefits of tuition waivers, university stipend, and progression on the school district salary scale are taken into consideration.

Graduate interns are selected from a group of applicants based upon their cumulative grade point average, prior success in student teaching and methodology courses, and their recommendations from cooperating teachers, university student teaching supervisors, and public school and university faculty members with whom they have previously worked.

Beginning teacher component. All beginning elementary class-room teachers who are not graduate interns (approximately one hundred fifteen teachers) also receive systematic, structured, weekly support within their classrooms from excellent veteran teachers who serve as clinical support teachers. Moreover, experienced teachers who are new to the school system or who are significantly changing grades or teaching areas receive limited support pertaining to the policies and procedures of the school district.

All program participants receive a monthly newsletter that includes a calendar of events, teaching ideas, and professional articles related to beginning teaching, which is written by clinical support teachers. Beginning teachers have the further opportunity to obtain university course credit at a reduced tuition rate by participating in bimonthly study groups led by clinical support teachers. The content for this guided study is suggested by beginning teachers based upon their current classroom experiences.

Clinical support teacher component. Excellent veteran teachers are released from their teaching duties for a period of two years, with full pay and benefits continuing, in order to work as clinical support teachers for the graduate interns, other beginning teachers, and experienced but new-to-the-system teachers. The term *clinical support teacher* is comparable to the terms *buddy teacher, guide teacher,* or *mentor teacher* in other support programs for beginning teachers. The assistance offered by the clinical support teachers is consultative and nonevaluative. It includes in-classroom teaching demonstration, materials collection, emotional and instructional support, and in-service workshops. The clinical support teachers also disseminate district-generated information and serve as program liaisons to building principals and the program director. They write and distribute a monthly newsletter for beginning teachers entitled "The Link," and they also lead bimonthly study groups for beginning teachers.

The clinical support teachers become adjunct faculty at the university with library, athletic facility, and cultural event privileges. Furthermore, they receive a tuition waiver for six semester hours at the university in order to attend courses that contribute to their own professional development.

Approximately one hundred thirty elementary teachers in sixty-five schools receive teacher induction support each year in the APS/UNM teacher induction program. Accordingly, each clinical support teacher has a client load of approximately sixteen beginning teachers.

Program director component. The teacher induction program is coordinated and directed by a university faculty member. The program director's general responsibilities include program administration, teaching courses for graduate interns and clinical support teachers, and acting as a liaison between the university and the public schools. As a university faculty member, the program director also engages in research, evaluation, and dissemination of information related to teacher induction.

Program Funding

A distinguishing feature of the APS/UNM Teacher Induction Program is a personnel exchange that allows the full-time clinical support teachers to be released from teaching in order to assist all of the approximately 130 beginning teachers in the school district at no additional cost to the school district. Figure 3.2 illustrates this unique, no additional cost exchange of personnel. Box A represents the sum of money ordinarily spent by the school district in order to staff fourteen elementary classrooms, assuming that each of these teachers receives the mean salary in the district. The remaining three boxes (B+C+D) show an alternative distribution of the same dollar amount, which when added together do not exceed the dollar amount represented in box A.

Figure 3.2
NO ADDITIONAL COST EXCHANGE FORMULA FOR THE
COLLABORATIVE PUBLIC SCHOOL/UNIVERSITY TEACHER
INDUCTION PROGRAM

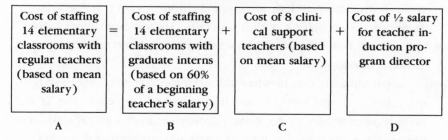

More specifically, the school district places fourteen graduate interns as full-time teachers into fourteen elementary classrooms. The graduate interns are paid a stipend equal to 60 percent of a beginning teacher's salary. The school system releases eight veteran teachers from teaching in order to work full time in inducting all of the district's new teachers. The salary and benefits for clinical support teachers continue as if they were teaching. Box D represents residual money from the exchange of personnel services that is used to defray one-half of the program director's salary.

Lessons Learned From Experience

The APS/UNM collaborative induction program has evolved over the past seven years. During this time the progrm has been evaluated both formatively and summatively (Odell in press). What follows is an overview of the lessons that have been learned about putting a successful collaborative induction program into place. These lessons pertain to (a) the selection, preparation, and compensation of clinical support teachers; (b) the necessity of separating assistance to the beginning teachers from their assessment; (c) the value of elaborating support beyond that offered by the clinical support teachers; and (d) the benefits of collaborations between school systems and university teacher educators.

Selection of Clinical Support Teachers

Experience has helped to identify those characteristics of veteran teachers that make them successful clinical support teachers. These characteristics serve as useful criteria when selecting support teachers and have been fully elaborated for that purpose elsewhere (Odell 1989a, 1990a). A brief overview of these criteria follows.

Demonstrated excellence in teaching. Clinical support teachers serve as role models for beginning teachers and, therefore, must be excellent classroom teachers.

Demonstrated excellence in working with adults. An excellent classroom teacher of children will not necessarily be an excellent clinical support teacher. Because clinical support teachers work to assist other adults, they should evince skill in interacting and communicating with adults.

Demonstrated sensitivity to the viewpoints of others. Since clinical support teachers are confident, competent teachers with extensive teaching experience they have the potential of being directive and proscriptive in working with beginning teachers. However, clinical support teachers must be able instead to establish a climate in which beginning teachers' strengths are recognized, viewpoints are respected, and self-identified needs are central to the support offered.

Demonstrated willingness to be an active and open learner. While clinical support teachers are presumed to be knowledgeable about teaching, they still need to be open to learning about strategies for working with beginning teachers and about the content and theory of teacher induction.

Demonstrated competence in social and public relations. Clinical support teachers interact with a variety of personalities inasmuch as they work with beginning teachers in several different schools. Part of the clinical support teacher's role is to adapt to the beginning teachers and school principals so as to engender positive professional and personal interactions among them.

Preparation of Support Teachers

The importance of preparing clinical support teachers arises from the previously stated presumption that even excellent veteran classroom teachers have limited experience in working with adults and may not a priori have all of the skills necessary to support beginning teachers. Odell (1990a, 1990b) has elsewhere described how to prepare clinical support teachers. In the APS/UNM program this is mainly done in weekly seminars with the program director. Ten seminar topics constitute the essential content necessary for preparing clinical support teachers to work effectively with beginning teachers. They include rationale for teacher induction programs, stages of teacher development, concerns of beginning teachers, fostering self-esteem in beginning teachers, fostering self-reliance in beginning teachers, working with adult learners, teacher mentoring, classroom observation and conferencing skills, teacher reflection and teacher coaching.

During the weekly seminars with the program director, clinical support teachers review articles related to the topics above and participate in activities that help to define more clearly the strategies for assisting beginning teachers. Case studies, role playing, and lively discussions constitute part of the clinical support teachers' ongoing study during their weekly seminar. The seminar also provides a context in which clinical support teachers can support one another in their own roles. This "support for support teachers" is a particularly important dimension of the weekly seminar.

Compensation for Clinical Support Teachers

There are obvious intrinsic benefits to being a clinical support teacher that often motivate veteran teachers to become involved in a collaborative teacher induction program. However, in addition to the intrinsic satisfactions derived from supporting colleagues, it is useful to provide clinical support teachers with extrinsic compensation in recognition of the added responsibilities that they assume. As already noted, in the APS/UNM collaborative teacher induction program, veteran teachers are released completely from classroom teaching and provided with tuition waivers so that they may advance their study of the teaching and learning processes. Other possible compensation might include additional salary or funding to travel to educational conferences. It would appear that the form of the added compensation is not so important as is the explicit recognition that in a teacher induction program, clinical support teachers assume the major responsibility for fostering our next generation of teachers.

Separation of Assistance and Assessment

As programs in teacher induction are designed, an important issue to be resolved is whether clinical support teachers should only offer assistance to beginning teachers or whether they should also assess beginning teachers' performances (Feiman-Nemser, Odell & Lawrence 1988, Odell in press). Both research and past experience suggest that it is important to separate teacher induction support from the evaluation of teaching. Consider that beginning teachers are often uncomfortable with those in evaluative positions and are reluctant to discuss their concerns, thereby denying themselves the assistance that they need (Fox & Singletary 1986, Odell 1987b). Moreover, beginning teachers appreciate the "beneficial feedback" that they receive from clinical support teachers, but only so long as these "friendly critics" are not in a formal evaluative role (Huffman & Leak 1986).

In the Albuquerque Public Schools all formal teaching evaluation of graduate interns and other beginning teachers is carried out by the school principal. Accordingly, the assistance offered to first-year teachers by the APS/UNM Teacher Induction Program is not compromised by being integrated with an evaluative function.

Elaboration of Support Services

Although clinical support teachers undoubtedly provide the most influential interventions in a teacher induction program (Huling-
Austin, Barnes & Smith 1985), teacher induction programs should
strive to be comprehensive by elaborating upon what the clinical support teachers offer to beginning teachers. For example, elaborated
support might involve the school district's staff development office
offering comprehensive orientations to beginning teachers at the start
of the school year or workshops targeting beginning teachers as part
of an in-service training program.

   Three elaborations of support that have been particularly useful
and popular among beginning teachers in the APS/UNM program are
beginning teacher self-study groups, beginning teacher visitations to
classrooms, and a newsletter written particularly for beginning teachers. The self-study groups provide a context for small groups of beginning teachers to discuss common interests and to share teaching
ideas with other beginning teachers. Visits to classrooms provide beginning teachers with models of instruction and ideas for provisioning
their learning environments. The newsletters communicate district
information, instructional strategies, and materials of particular relevance to beginning teachers.

Collaboration

A final, but important, lesson that is highlighted by a collaborative
teacher induction program is that collaborations between public
schools and universities can work well and should be encouraged. In
the context of teacher induction, such collaborations combine the
theoretical and research expertise of university faculty with the applied and clinical teaching expertise of public school personnel so as
to optimize the development of beginning teachers. Moreover, after a
collaborative induction program has been in place for an extended
period of time, as has the APS/UNM program, there is a progression in
which prior beginning teachers and interns become clinical support

teachers and prior clinical support teachers become principals. In this manner the theory and practice of collaborative teacher induction become more integrated into the fabric of the school to the benefit of all succeeding beginning teachers.

Promising Outcomes of Teacher Induction

Formal interviews, questionnaires, and structured observations have been used in order to conduct a summative evaluation of the various components of the APS/UNM collaborative teacher induction program. These evaluations have served to identify some important benefits of the teacher induction program to the various program participants and to the participating schools and university.

Benefits to Beginning Teachers

In a questionnaire administered at the end of each program year from 1985 to 1989, beginning teachers responded on a five-point scale to questions about the teacher induction program. For all items on the questionnaire, the closer the response was to five, the more favorable the response was to the teacher induction program. Mean responses were calculated across the five years for each item.

Overall, beginning teachers reported that their involvement in the teacher induction program was very positive (4.4) and that it significantly impacted their professional growth as teachers (4.4). Specifically, they reported that clinical support teachers were available when needed (4.8), helpful (4.4), supportive (4.8), and offered constructive feedback (4.3).

In a separate follow-up study (Odell 1989b), fourth-year teachers were asked to what extent their previous involvement in the teacher induction program had contributed to their attitudes about teaching and about themselves as teachers. After four years the teachers reported a continuing positive influence (4.3) from their prior teacher induction experiences.

A study was conducted in order to reveal what changes occur in beginning teachers' concerns across their first year of teaching (Odell 1987a). Within the collaborative teacher induction program, beginning teachers exhibit personal concerns early in the first school year but move toward concerns related to teaching and the impact of their teaching on students as the school year progresses. In a related vein, the various categories of support that beginning teachers request and that clinical support teachers offer to beginning teachers in a teacher induction context have been identified (Odell 1986, Odell, Loughlin & Ferraro 1987). Unlike beginning teachers who are not receiving teacher induction support (Veenman 1984), beginning teachers in a teacher induction program focus more on instructional issues than on issues related to the disciplining of students. These studies also document the importance of offering emotional support to beginning teachers.

Benefits to Clinical Support Teachers

Program interviews with clinical support teachers have suggested that among the primary benefits that accrue to them are increased personal confidence, broadened perspectives about the school district, increased knowledge about teaching and learning, and enhanced communication skills. These benefits are similar to those found for support teachers in other teacher induction programs (e.g., Hawk 1987) and reinforce the long-held belief that those who teach teachers become themselves better teachers.

Benefits to Principals

Principals have also provided information about the impact of teacher induction. A five-point scale item questionnaire was administered to principals at the end of each program year from 1985 to 1989. Principals viewed their participation in the program as very favorable (4.7). They saw regular classroom visitations to beginning teachers by clinical support teachers as very important (4.9), and described the support teachers' communication with the principal as useful (4.6). In general, principals expressed the opinion that beginning teachers benefited greatly from the assistance offered to them by clinical support teachers.

Interestingly, the principals observed that the benefits of teacher inductions generalized to their entire teaching staff. Specifically, principals stated that the presence of the teacher induction program positively influenced the atmosphere in their schools by emphasizing teacher interactions and collaborations. This "multiplier effect" of teacher induction is an unexpected but welcome positive influence on people beyond those directly participating in the program. An additional benefit reported by principals is that the assistance offered by clinical support teachers somewhat relieves them of the burden that they carry when they do not have the time to interact as frequently as they would like with beginning teachers.

Benefits to the Program Director

From the perspective of the program director, close interactions with graduate interns, other beginning teachers, and clinical support teachers provide a context within which to link the theory of teaching to the practice of working with children. The induction program also provides the program director with a clinical laboratory for the study of beginning teacher needs and the development of beginning teachers who are undergoing induction support.

Benefits to the Schools

The benefits of teacher induction programs to the public schools are isomorphic with the benefits described for the program participants. Basically, the school district is positively affected by having as employees satisfied and competent beginning teachers. A particularly significant benefit to the schools is that teacher induction may enhance beginning teacher retention. Teacher retention studies have shown that nationally up to 40 percent of beginning teachers leave the profession within four years (Schlechty & Vance 1983). Similar four-year attrition surveys from the program's home state suggest that attrition is 45.4 percent in New Mexico (New Mexico State Department of Education 1988).

In a follow-up study of the APS/UNM program (Odell 1989b), it was found that the four-year attrition rates for beginning teachers who had received induction support were substantially below both the national and state attrition rates. Specifically, of 160 beginning teachers followed up four years later, only six (4.3 percent) of the 141 teachers who were located had resigned from teaching. If it is assumed that all of the teachers who were not located during the follow-up period had resigned from teaching, which seems unlikely, the four-year attrition rate of the entire cohort of teachers who have received previous induction support would still be only 15.6 percent. Which is more, 88 percent of the fourth-year graduates of the induction program reported that they intended to remain in teaching or to move into educational administration over the ensuing five years. Were these predictions to be accurate, these teachers would evince a significantly lower than usual dropout rate, which is generally assumed to approximate 6 percent per year for experienced teachers (Schlechty & Vance 1983).

Benefits to the University

The traditional context of university involvement with teachers is in preservice preparation. By collaborating with a school district in inducting beginning teachers, a university extends its involvement into the teachers' initial year of teaching and beyond. It seems apparent that any university that offers teacher training directly benefits from having applied experiences in classrooms. There seems to be no more salient way to do this than through a collaborative teacher induction program.

Note

1. The Albuquerque Public Schools/University of New Mexico Elementary Teacher Induction Program received the Distinguished

Achievement Award from the American Association of Colleges For Teacher Education in 1985. Additionally, the program has been targeted for study by the National Center for Research in Teacher Education at Michigan State University and by the Educational Testing Service. The authors acknowledge Professor Keith Auger of the University of New Mexico who provided the funding conceptualization for this program, which more recently has been extended to the secondary level.

References

Adams, R. D. A look at changes in teacher perceptions and behavior across time. *Journal of Teacher Education, 33*(4), 40–43.

Berliner, D. C. (1986). In pursuit of the expert pedagogue. *Educational Researcher, 15*(7), 5–13.

——— (1988). The development of expertise in pedagogy. Charles W. Hunt Memorial Lecture presented at the annual meeting of the American Association of Colleges for Teacher Education, New Orleans, LA.

Brooks, D. M. (1986). *Richardson new teacher induction program: Final data analyses and report.* Richardson, TX: Richardson IMSD (ERIC No. ED278 627).

Cogan, M. (1975). Current issues in the education of teachers. In K. Ryan, ed., *Teacher education, Seventy-fourth yearbook of the National Society for the Study of Education.* Chicago, IL: University of Chicago Press.

Feiman-Nemser, S.; Odell, S. J.; and Lawrence, D. (1988). Induction programs and the professionalization of teachers: Two views. *Colloquy, 1*(2), 11–19.

Fox, S. M.; and Singletary, T. J. (1986). Deductions about supportive induction. *Journal of Teacher Education, 37*(1), 12–15.

Fuller, F. F. (1969). Concerns of teachers: A developmental conceptualization. *American Educational Research Journal, 6,* 207–226.

Glassberg, S. (1979). A developmental model for the beginning teacher. In K. R. Howey, ed., *Toward meeting the needs of the beginning teacher.* Lansing, MI: Midwest Teacher Corps Network.

Gray, W. A.; and Gray, M. M. (1985). Synthesis of research on mentoring beginning teachers. *Educational Leadership, 43*(3), 37–43.

Hawk, P. (1987). Beginning teacher programs: Benefits for the experienced educator. *Action in Teacher Education, 8*(4), 59–63.

Huffman, G.; and Leak, S. (1986). Beginning teachers' perceptions of mentors. *Journal of Teacher Education, 37*(1), 22–25.

Huling-Austin, L. (1987). Teacher induction. In D. M. Brooks, ed., *Teacher induction: A new beginning.* Reston, VA: Association of Teacher Educators.

———— (1990). Teacher induction programs and internships. In W. R. Houston, ed., *Handbook of Research on Teacher Education.* New York: MacMillan.

Huling-Austin, L.; Barnes, S.; and Smith, J. (1985). A research-based development program for beginning teachers. Paper presented at the annual meeting of the American Education Research Association, Chicago, IL.

Katz, L. L. (1972). Developmental stages of preschool teachers. *Elementary School Journal, 73,* 50–54.

Lortie, D. D. (1975). *Schoolteacher: A sociological study.* Chicago, IL: University of Chicago Press.

New Mexico State Department of Education. (1988). *Preliminary report: New Mexico enrollment and teacher needs projections.* Evaluation, Testing, and Data Management Unit.

Odell, S. J. (1986). Induction support of new teachers: A functional approach. *Journal of Teacher Education, 37*(1), 26–29.

———— (1987a). Stages of concern of beginning teachers in a collaborative internship induction program. Paper presented at the annual meeting of the Association of Teacher Educators, Houston, TX.

———— (1987b). Teacher induction: Rationale and issues. In D. Brooks, ed., *Teacher induction: A new beginning.* Reston, VA: Association of Teacher Education.

———— (1989a). Developing support programs for beginning teachers. In L. Huling-Austin, S. Odell, P. Ishler, R. Kay, and R. Edelfelt, *Beginning teacher assistance programs.* Reston, VA: Association of Teacher Educators.

———— (1989b). Long-term effects of teacher induction: A four-year follow-up study. Paper presented at the annual meeting of the Association of Teacher Educators, St. Louis, MO.

———— (1990a). *Mentoring teachers.* Washington, D.C.: National Education Association.

————(1990b). Support for new teachers. In T. M. Bey and C. T. Holmes, eds., *Mentoring: Developing successful new teachers.* Reston, VA: Association of Teacher Educators.

————(1990c). Teacher induction: A collaborative program that works. *Journal of Staff Development, 11*(4), 12–16.

————(In press). Evaluating mentoring programs. In T. Bey, ed., *Principles of mentoring.* Reston, VA: Association of Teacher Educators.

Odell, S. J.; Loughlin, C. E.; and Ferraro, D. P. (1987). Functional approach to identification of new teacher needs in an induction context. *Action in Teacher Education, 8*(4), 51–57.

Roth, R. A. (1986). Emergency certificates, missing assignment of teachers, and other "dirty little secrets." *Phi Delta Kappan, 67*(10), 725–727.

Ryan, K. (1986). *The induction of new teachers.* Phi Delta Kappa Fastback No. 237. Bloomington, IN: Phi Delta Kappa Educational Foundation.

Schlechty, P.; and Vance, V. (1983). Recruitment, selection and retention: The shape of the teaching force. *Elementary School Journal, 83,* 469–487.

Veenman, S. (1984). Perceived problems of beginning teachers. *Review of Education Research, 54*(2), 143–178.

4. The North Country Mentor/Intern Teacher Program:
A Rural Consortium

NICHOLAS G. STUPIANSKY
MICHAEL P. WOLFE

Wolfe and Stupiansky report on the origins and functioning of a consortium involving collaboration among several small, isolated, mostly rural school districts and a branch of the State University in Northern New York. The roles of various participants are explained; resulting benefits for mentoring and collaboration are reported.

How beginning teachers learn to teach has been the subject of considerable speculation and myth, but little systematic description or inquiry (Hammond 1984). Recently, however, this area has emerged as a major focus for research and practice in teacher education.

Teacher Induction: The Concept and The Need

Most research in teacher education has focused upon the theory and practice during the preservice phase. The induction phase of teaching, the initial one to three years, has not been studied in depth, despite the fact that the beginning teacher faces numerous new challenges the first few years (Veenman 1984). Nationally, it has been estimated that approximately 15 percent of new teachers leave after their first year of teaching, compared to the overall turnover rate of 6 percent (Schlechty & Vance 1983). Of all beginning teachers, 40 to 50 percent will leave during the first seven years of their career (Huling-Austin 1985).

The first year of teaching is especially important because of the significant impact it has on the development and profile of a person's teaching career. Macdonald (1980), Feiman-Nemser (1983), and others have argued that the first year is the critical year of teaching, determining whether a person will stay in the teaching profession and what type of teacher that person will become. In describing these first years of a teacher's professional life, Bush (1966) says, "Here he learns his role, internalizes the basic values of the teacher's culture, forms his conceptions and standards that will strongly influence his behavior for years to come" (p. 7).

There is ample evidence (e.g., Grant & Zeichner 1984) that the beginning teacher faces many hurdles in attempting to successfully negotiate that first year of teaching. Horror stories of beginning teacher problems and crises, both professional and personal, fill entire books (e.g., Ryan et al. 1980). It seems apparent that, in the past, many beginning teachers have lacked support and guidance during the initial teaching years. Indeed, entry into the profession was sudden, with the beginning teacher assuming many of the same responsibilities as the veteran. Lortie (1966) refers to this experience as the "sink or swim" Robinson Crusoe approach. Lortie (1975) says that teaching seems to be the only profession where "the beginner becomes fully responsible from the first working day and performs the same tasks as a twenty-five year veteran" (p. 72).

The present New York State system of teacher certification, like many other states, allows for a teacher candidate to be provisionally certified, employed, and then permanently certified after the completion of a master's degree and two years of teaching experience. Thus, inexperienced first-year teachers enter the classroom with full responsibility as practicing professionals with little support or guidance.

Although faced with feelings of isolation, some beginning teachers report a useful and constant source of support from fellow teachers. This support is articulated through informal mentor-protege relationships established between a beginning teacher and an experienced colleague. However, this informal support is not always present when needed, unless built into the culture of a school. The culture and accompanying traditions, mores, and ceremonies including the actual school setting can also present special advantages or disadvantages. Teaching in a rural school setting, in particular, can intensify the feelings of isolation.

Located in the northeast corner of upstate New York, the State University of New York (SUNY) at Plattsburgh is within sixty miles of nineteen small, rural school districts. The New York State Legislative Commission of Rural Resources (1985) has identified this upstate New York region as suffering from a list of disadvantages: lack of availability of quality teaching personnel due to low salaries, limited program and staff, insufficient career guidance for students, problems presented by geographic isolation of large numbers of the rural population, limited summer education, and lack of state-of-the-art communications technology.

This list of disadvantages inherent in some small rural school situations could contribute to potential drawbacks regarding the recruitment and induction of new teachers. One problem is attracting high-quality teachers to rural areas. Also, the pool of available teaching positions is limited in rural areas, thus, beginning teachers may be isolated even further. Differentiated staff development programs, which address the needs of beginning teachers, are difficult to deliver due to the relatively small numbers of new teachers in rural areas.

Thus, the North Country Mentor/Intern Teacher Project was born out of a real need to attract and retain high-quality beginning teachers and to provide differentiated staff development programs for retaining these new teachers. Assisting the transition of the beginning teacher into the teaching profession became the primary goal of the North Country Mentor/Intern Teacher Project.

Other primary goals of the North Country Mentor/Intern program include the following: to improve the teaching performance of the beginning teacher; to enhance the retention of high-quality beginning teachers; to maximize the utilization of professional resources available in the rural, North Country regional area; and to develop a regional decision-making organization to determine common needs of mentor/intern projects and to address those needs through a comprehensive training program.

Realizing these goals meant challenging the prevailing modes of in-service delivery systems sponsored by several different stakeholder groups and developing a collaborative system for meeting the needs of beginning teachers.

Key Stakeholders in In-service Education in New York State

In New York State, as in many other states, there are multiple parties which are competing for the responsibility to deliver staff development for in-service teachers. For example, in New York State, the following six interest groups have been visible in their attempts to address the needs of in-service teachers: school districts, Board of Cooperative Educational Services (BOCES), teacher centers, teacher unions and associations, the State Education Department, and institutions of higher education.

School districts. Many school districts, particularly larger school districts, coordinate, staff, and deliver in-service programs for their teachers. However, the majority of school districts, particularly the smaller school districts, do not have the resources nor the staff available to offer extensive in-service teacher education programs for beginning teachers. These districts often resort to hiring outside consultants to provide one-shot in-service programs or rely on other agencies and organizations within the state to provide such programs.

BOCES. The Board of Cooperative Educational Services (a regional network of school districts) does not appear to have a clear mission with regard to the professional development of beginning teachers. Many BOCES do provide occasional topical workshops for teachers in their geographical area, but there is confusion about what role it plays in ongoing in-service education to the districts it represents.

Teacher centers. State-funded teacher centers have played an active role in in-service programs, particularly within the last five years. Currently there seems to be a need to expand the role that teacher centers play in the professional development of new teachers, especially in the practical day-to-day activities of classrooms.

Teacher unions/associations. The New York State United Teachers (NYSUT), the New York National Education Association, and other teacher organizations promote professional development activities in such areas as teacher effectiveness, cooperative learning, and other programs with immediate and practical values.

State Education Department. The New York State Education Department sponsors regional and statewide conferences to introduce new concepts and innovations to school districts throughout the state. Recent topics include effective schools, school climate, and whole language to name a few.

Institutions of higher education. The primary concern of colleges and universities has been to provide postbaccalaureate programs for teachers attempting to earn permanent certification. These programs service mainly beginning teachers who are involved in the initial five years of teacher education. Frequently, college and university faculty also provide one-shot professional development workshops. Many of these are delivered as entrepreneurial activities.

Each of the aforementioned stakeholders is vying for access to and the control (however limited this may be) of the continued professional development of teachers. Can the involvement of so many individual entities or stakeholders be in the best interests of teachers and of the profession?

Partnerships

One answer to the confusing multiplicity of roles and duality of functions is the establishment of partnerships that focus on mutual goals. Sirotnik and Goodlad (1988) have defined a partnership as a "mutually collaborative arrangement between equal partners working together to meet self-interests while solving common problems... a form of institutional collaboration that rarely [if ever] has occurred in practice" (p. vii).

Partnerships are not new in education. In fact, one only has to search educational journals and other publications within the past few years to find evidence of growing popularity. Within school partnerships (Sirotnik & Goodlad 1988), between school partnerships (Goodlad 1986), business and school partnerships (United States Office of Education 1985), and university and school partnerships (Wolfe & Charland 1989) have been started across the country. Within New York State, university and school collaboration in math and science education as well as other areas was the focus of a recent issue of *The Voice* (1989).

New York State has responded by instituting new certification regulations which promote increased liberal arts credits and an induction year utilizing a mentor/intern model. However, mentoring will only work if a partnership is formed with common agreements and focus by each of the stakeholders having access to ongoing professional development. Unless this common ideal/mission/vision is shared by all stakeholders, its success will be threatened.

The New York State Mentor/Intern Teacher Program

In 1986, the state of New York responded to the unique character and importance of the induction years, particularly the first year of teaching, by passing legislation entitled, "Mentor Teacher-Internship Program." The purpose of this legislation was to foster the development of Mentor Teacher-Internship Programs in school districts to support first-year probationary teachers. The process involved school districts submitting competititve applications to the State Education Department describing plans to develop and implement Mentor Teacher-Internship Programs. For the years 1986–87, 1987–88, 1988–89, and 1989–90, the State Legislature appropriated $4 million, $8 million, $10+ million, and $12.5 million, respectively, to be distributed through these competitive grants to local school districts. Twenty-four programs were funded for 1986–87, twenty-nine programs were funded for 1987–88, fifty programs were funded in 1988–89, and seventy-one programs were funded for 1989–90 (see figure 4.1). The aim of the legislation was that eventually the funded programs might serve as prototypes for other districts in subsequent years. Thus, a vehicle has been established to capitalize on the informal mentor-intern relationships that often exist in schools by providing the structure and resources to formalize this mentoring process by matching eligible beginning teachers with master teachers.

Eligible interns are full-time teachers in their first year of service in a certification area, holding a provisional certificate or temporary license. Eligible mentors must be selected by a local selection committee which is comprised of a majority of teachers chosen by the recognized local teachers union. At the present time, the internship is not a requirement for initial state certification, but it will be mandated by 1993 for all new teachers. The internship is not formally linked with institutional preparation. Financial aid is available to participating local education agencies for such purposes as release time for teachers (20 percent for interns and 10 percent for mentors for each intern served), training, and materials.

The North Country Mentor/Intern Teacher Consortium

In 1986, a collaborative effort was initiated by the Plattsburgh City School District in cooperation with the North Country Teacher Resource Center and the Center for Teacher Education at the State University of New York (SUNY), Plattsburgh. This effort resulted in a successful attempt to obtain state funding as one of the twenty-four intern teacher/mentor training projects funded through a competitive grant process in New York during 1986–87. Because of the success of this collaborative effort, the Center for Teacher Education at SUNY-Plattsburgh and the North Country Teacher Resource Center became partners with Plattsburgh City Schools, Peru School District, Ausable Valley School District, and Saranac School District to create the North

Figure 4.1

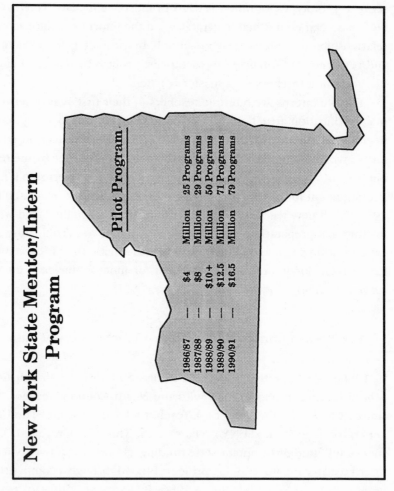

New York State Mentor/Intern Program

Pilot Program

1986/87	—	$4	Million	25 Programs
1987/88	—	$8	Million	29 Programs
1988/89	—	$10+	Million	50 Programs
1989/90	—	$12.5	Million	71 Programs
1990/91	—	$16.5	Million	79 Programs

Country Mentor/Intern Teacher Regional Consortium. These school districts represented four of only twenty-nine projects funded for 1987–88 in the state of New York. In 1988–89, Plattsburgh City, Peru, Saranac, and Moriah were part of the consortium. In 1989–90, Plattsburgh City, Peru, Saranac, and the Clinton-Essex-Warren-Washington BOCES comprised the consortium. (See figure 4.2.)

Figure 4.2

Consortium Organizational Chart

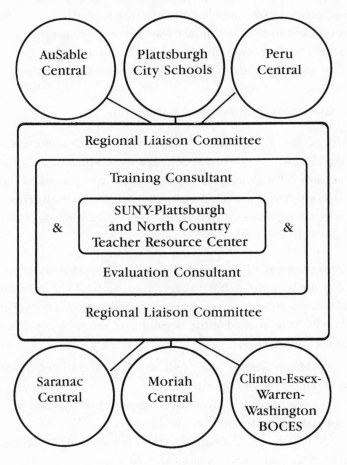

The purpose of this consortium is to maximize access and utilization of professional resources (human and material) that are available in rural northern New York. Through this consortium arrangement, multiple pairs of mentors and interns in four school districts are provided training and supervision via a partnership with SUNY-Plattsburgh teacher education faculty. The consortium provides a vehicle for common orientation sessions, comprehensive needs assessments, training sessions that address collective needs, strategy sessions for implementing local activities, and evaluation sessions. The consortium also facilitates regional and local "turnkey" training activities and provides assistance for meeting district and individual needs of mentors and interns. A summer training program for mentors and bimonthly regional consortium workshops enable participants from each district to share ideas, resources, and expertise (see figure 4.3).

Needs Assessment, Training, and Evaluation

The process for needs assessment, training, and evaluation at the district and consortium levels was designed to be efficient and comprehensive. SUNY-Plattsburgh faculty members, who served as district training consultants, provided a formal linkage with each school district to tailor the training activities to the separate needs of the districts and individual mentor-intern pairs.

Needs assessment. A comprehensive need assessment process served as the basis for all training activities. Both formal and informal means were devised to assess the intern and mentor needs. Formal instruments were utilized at the beginning of the program. These included the following:

1. Myers-Briggs Type Indicator—analyze operational styles (mentors and interns)
2. Teacher Stress Inventory—identify personal and professional stressors (mentors and interns)
3. Effective Teaching Instrument—assess teaching knowledge and skills (mentors and interns)

Figure 4.3
*Timeline Overview of Local and Regional
Mentor/Intern Program in the North Country*

June 10	Mentor Eligibility/Interest List	Steering Committee Meetings
June 24	Mentors Identified for Summer Institute	
Aug 29–Sept 2	Summer Institute-Mentor Training	
Aug 31	Assignment of Mentors to Interns by Supt.	
Sept 6	Interns Needs Assessments Administered	
Sept 6	District & Building Orientation	
Sept 19	Regional Program Orientation	

Sept 15	Mentor & Intern Activities Identify & Address Needs at District Level	Consortium Liaison Meetings Regional Quarterly Training Meetings	District Training Steering Committee Meetings	Documentation of all Activities Evaluation Plan Implemented

May 4	Local Program Evaluation Review
May 18	Regional Program Evaluation Meeting
July 7	Program Report to Board of Education
July 31	Program Report to SED

(*continued*)

Figure 4.3 (*continued*)

PROGRAM IMPLEMENTATION AREA	FACILITATOR			
	District	*Network [NCTRC]*	*Training Consultant*	*Evaluation Consultant*
1. Mentor Eligibility List	X			
2. Summer Mentor Institute		X	X	X
3. Intern Selection	X			
4. Intern/Mentor Matches	X			
5. Needs Assessment	X	X	X	X
6. District Orientation	X			
7. Initial Meetings of Mentor and Intern	X			
8. Program Orientation at Districts	X		X	X
9. Fall Retreat	X	X	X	X
10. Liaison Committee Meetings		X		
11. Bimonthly Training Meetings		X	X	X
12. Quarterly Newsletter	X	X	X	X
13. Mentor/Intern "Work Plan Activities"	X			
14. District Training	X		X	
15. District Reports and Evaluation	X			X
16. Regional Reports and Evaluation		X		X

4. Beginning Teacher Needs Assessment Inventory—clarify areas of need or concern (interns)

5. Mentor Teacher Needs Assessment Inventory—clarify areas of need or concern (mentors)

6. Counseling Assessment—identify counseling skills and styles (mentors)

7. Training Session Assessment—monthly input on needs (mentors and interns).

Informal techniques included ongoing mentor/intern conferences, seminar discussions, self-evaluations, peer coaching, videotape feedback, professional dialogues, and information provided by the local district steering committee members and principals. Based on the information obtained from the initial and ongoing needs assessments and the related literature on the documented needs of beginning teachers (e.g., Veenman 1984, Gowie 1986), intern and mentor needs were identified and were incorporated into a Mentor/Intern Action

Plan for use by mentors and interns to cooperatively identify intern needs and ways to address these needs. This plan provided a continuous process for monitoring the growth of the intern and evaluating the progress being made. Also, as new needs were expressed, the plan was modified and activities were developed to address these needs. Given the results of the needs assessment process, training activities were planned at the respective consortium, district, and mentor/intern team levels.

Training. Training activities were developed at the consortium level to address the common needs and concerns of mentors, interns, or both mentors and interns across school districts. Furthermore, district-level training activities were developed to address individual mentor and intern needs and concerns.

The training system facilitated the development of the beginning teacher at three levels: (a) technical/information assistance, that is, student referral forms, faculty committees, etc.; (b) personal support structure, that is, peer counseling about grading, dealing with parents, etc.; (c) cognitive/analytical dimension, that is, what teaching strategy is appropriate for a specific situation, etc.

Training focused on the mentors' and interns' needs and included a variety of topics: dimensions of a mentor's role, stages of teacher growth, adult development and learning concepts, district orientation and staff development programs, group building/dyadic encounters, effective teaching skills, substitute/replacement teacher training, counseling skills, peer coaching, interactive supervision, teaching and learning styles, classroom management and discipline, analysis of teaching, curriculum development and teaching methods, and other additional training as needed.

Evaluation. A comprehensive evaluation plan was an integral component of the project. Both qualitative and quantitative types of data were obtained throughout the project in an attempt to judge the project's impact and overall effectiveness. Additionally, since the project entailed a number of equally important dimensions (including the attitude and performance changes related to the interns and mentors; the relationships between the mentors, interns, replacement teachers, colleagues, and district consultant; the impact and effectiveness of various training components; etc.), the evaluation approach was multifaceted concentrating on these various subdimensions utilizing both a preordinate and responsive evaluation design.

Program documentation and sources of evaluation data included the following items:

1. Pre/Post Needs Assessment
2. Implementation of Mentor/Intern Action Plans
3. Consortium Training Activities
4. Mentor and Intern Written Final Project Evaluations
5. Mentor and Intern Summative Interviews
6. College Connector Summative Interviews
7. Feedback from Advisory Committees, Building Administrators, and Replacement Teachers

The combination of these evaluation activities was designed to assess the impact of the Mentor Teacher-Internship Project and the goals established for the project.

Project Outcomes

Project outcomes from the first four years are overwhelmingly positive. Not only were the attitudes and performance of beginning teachers significantly improved, the program also enhanced and energized the careers of several veteran mentor teachers. The professional growth expressed by the mentors involved was equivalent to the gains made by the beginning teachers.

Success of the North Country Mentor/Intern Consortium was verified through a number of sources. The Beginning Teacher Needs Assessment Inventory was completed by all interns both at the beginning and at the conclusion of the program. The results of this instrument highlighted areas of needs and strengths as perceived by the interns.

An analysis was conducted comparing the pretest and posttest data to determine if the needs of the interns had been met during the program. One part of the inventory contained forty-one items related to teaching activities with which beginning teachers might want assistance. Interns were asked to respond to the forty-one items using a five-point Likert scale (ranging from no assistance needed [1], to definitely need assistance [5]). On nearly all of the forty-one items in the survey, the needs of the interns as expressed by the posttest data appeared to be partially or significantly reduced. There only existed seven items among the four school districts on which intern needs were not reduced. Four of these items involved issues related to cultural learners. It is very possible that the interns, at the beginning of the year, did not perceive a need in this area, but only after teaching a year did this need become known. At the consortium level, mean scores on all items reflected a decrease in intern needs at the conclusion of the project. Thus, it can be concluded, based on the results of this instrument, the Mentor/Intern Program and the training program associated with it were highly effective in meeting and satisfying the needs of the intern teachers in all four districts.

Mentors and interns were asked to respond to a six-page final evaluation form which focused on all of the objectives set forth in the initial grant proposal. Based on a summary of the mentor and intern comments, in combination with all the other data collected during the evaluation process, the program was very successful based on the degree to which these 'expected outcomes have been realized. All of the mentors, interns, principals, steering committee members, and program coordinators expressed much satisfaction with the Mentor/ Intern Program as it related to these objectives.

Interns were also asked to respond to a summative evaluation rating form focusing on the area of teaching skills. The intern evaluation form consisted of seven items: five rating scales and two short narrative statements. Four of the five rating scales asked interns to indicate how much the internship experience affected the following: instructional planning and management, effective classroom management, number and quality of skills in presenting subject matter, and number and quality of communication skills. Each of these four rating scales had seven response positions on a Likert scale, from -3 to $+3$.

The fifth rating scale had four response positions, from 0 to +3, and asked the intern to indicate how valuable the intern experience was. Average intern ratings on these five scales were +1.7, +1.6, +1.4, +1.7, +2.7. These ratings parallel, almost identically, the average statewide ratings of the 1986–87 Mentor/Intern Programs using the same rating form. The general tenor of the interns' comments was overwhelmingly positive. These data, in combination with the other evaluation data collected, provide further evidence that the program has worked successfully.

Program evaluations, solicited from building administrators and steering committee members, supported the positive perceptions of mentors and interns regarding the success of the project. Building administrators provided evidence to support the fact that teaching performance of the beginning teachers was enhanced by their involvement in the program.

There is overwhelming evidence that each of the program goals has been accomplished, that the participants and all those connected with the program are pleased with the outcomes, and that there remains a strong desire for continuation of District Mentor/Intern Programs and the Regional Consortium in succeeding years.

Related spin-offs from this project also have been evident. These include many benefits such as new district teacher orientation plans, curriculum development projects, peer coaching projects, and refreshing teacher leadership displayed by both mentors and interns. A summary of the project outcomes is listed below.

1) *Growth of interns:* (a) improved teaching performance of beginning teachers, (b) accelerated development as professionals, (c) increased retention of beginning teachers, (d) individualized teacher professional growth plan, (e) less stress, (f) more positive attitude, (g) greater use of North Country resources, (h) enhanced leadership skills, (i) teacher empowerment.

2) *Growth of mentors:* (a) improved teaching performance of mentor teachers, (b) improved mentoring skills,

(c) time to reflect on teaching, (d) revitalization of mentor teacher, (e) more positive attitude, (f) opportunity for various types of involvement.

3) *Other school district benefits:* (a) formalized support system, (b) orientation program for new faculty members, (c) school district and teacher networking, (d) replacement teacher training, (e) collaboration among teachers and administrators, (f) greater utilization of human and material educational resources within the North Country, (g) continued informal mentor/intern relationship beyond first year, (h) related projects by mentor/intern participants, (i) increased pool of professional expertise, (j) improved communication within district, (k) increased benefits to students.

The strength of the consortium model is that, while it maximizes the utilization of professional resources available to any one program in a rural area of New York State, it also allows for individual variability and flexibility among school district programs. The advantage of this model is that the school district can adopt the program goals, objectives, and activities offered by the consortium, and tailor the program to meet the district and individual mentor and intern needs. It combines multidistrict cooperation and flexibility in an efficient and cost-effective manner.

The partnership between the college and the school districts has been further enhanced. College involvement in induction activities with mentors and interns has further reduced the false dichotomy which exists between the preservice and in-service phases of the teacher education continuum.

A final outcome of the project is the comprehensive needs assessment and training process which has applicability to other sites. The development of a differentiated staff development program based on the real needs of beginning and mentor teachers has been successfully realized. A needs assessment process which produces a workable staff development action plan and is linked to appropriate and relevant training activities has helped to empower teachers at critical stages in their careers.

The College Connection

A critical component in the North Country Mentor/Intern Teacher Consortium is the college connection. Since the consortium involves multiple school districts, a faculty member in teacher education from SUNY-Plattsburgh serves as the college connector for each district. This linkage with individual districts enables specialized teacher development programs which are unique to the district or individual mentor/intern pairs. This also formalizes the relationship of the college with the teacher induction in-service programs of beginning teachers.

All needs assessment, training, and evaluation activities are coordinated by university faculty. These activities are designed to address the stated and perceived needs of mentors and interns on three levels: consortium level, school district level, and individual mentor/intern pair level.

The extent that SUNY-Plattsburgh is involved in the planning, delivery, and evaluation of the mentor/intern program is unparalleled throughout the state. Institutions of higher education were not included in the original legislation; rather local educational agencies (school districts or BOCES) were targeted as sponsoring agencies.

Issues to Consider

Several recurring issues provide a focus for continued improvement. These issues include the following areas: (a) procurement and preparation of replacement teachers, (b) the problem of scheduling release time, (c) the issue of time out of the classroom, and (d) communication and faculty perceptions. Each of these will be described briefly.

The time involved in the planning for and orientation of substitute and replacement teachers was frequently mentioned as the most frustrating aspect of the mentor/intern experience. This concern about the replacement teacher was more evident at the elementary level where the scheduling of release time was more difficult than at the secondary level where teachers were released one period per day. The best situation seemed to occur when the same replacement teacher was scheduled and committed to one classroom throughout the length of the program. Consistency and commitment from replacement teachers was the key. The ability to maintain a quality education program in the mentor's or intern's classroom was important for the program participants as well as for the students involved.

The problem of scheduling release time was also a concern. In several situations, the mentor and the intern had common class times and different release times. Thus, observing in each other's classrooms was sometimes difficult. In other situations where the mentor and intern shared a replacement teacher during different release times, teachers found it difficult to conference since the release times were not the same. Thus, the mentor and intern found themselves conferencing during evening hours or over the telephone. The use of one replacement teacher for one mentor/intern pair also made it difficult for both mentor and intern to attend training programs on the same day since another replacement teacher had to be obtained and prepared for the second classroom. This resulted in loss of consistency in the classroom and additional stress on teacher and students.

Another concern of the project participants was related to the issue of time out of the classroom. Tension exists between involvement in the mentor/intern program activities and the presence of the teacher in the classroom attending to the needs of the students. Both were important; both competed for time. Participants expressed a desire to begin the program much earlier in the year, or prior to the start of the year, so less time away from classrooms and students could be realized.

Lack of communication about the mentor/intern program and its related activities and the resulting faculty perceptions was a continuing concern. Mentors and interns often felt obligated to inform and defend the program to colleagues and parents. Participants viewed themselves in a defensive role attempting to justify to their colleagues the time involved in the program and their access to increased opportunities because of the program. Misperceptions of faculty colleagues endangered one of the programs and resulted in additional stress on program participants. Early program orientation for parents, faculty colleagues, building principals, and replacement teachers is a critical aspect of the program which needs to be addressed.

With the implementation and evolution of any new program, a number of issues or concerns are likely to surface. None of these issues present insurmountable problems; rather they stimulate continuous growth in building an exemplary mentoring program.

Conclusion

The culture of cooperation which characterizes the North Country Mentor/Intern Teacher Consortium is largely responsible for the continued success of the program. This spirit of cooperation, which was evident from the inception of the proposal, has pervaded all aspects of program delivery. A partnership and common understanding exists among all stakeholders in the project: school administration, teacher unions, regional teacher center, and the university.

A critical aspect of the program continues to be differentiating the evaluative role of the building administrator from the supportive and professional growth role of the mentor. Confidentiality between mentor and intern is respected because of the valued relationship between the mentor and intern teachers. This healthy relationship is continually enhanced through systematic needs-based training activities which have enabled both mentor and intern teachers to grow personally and professionally. In rural, upstate New York, beginning teachers are discovering a smooth transition into teaching because many resources enhancing their growth have been connected through the North Country Mentor/Intern Teacher Consortium.

References

Bush, R. N. (1966). In National Education Association, *The real world of the beginning teacher.* Washington, D.C.: NEA.

Feiman-Nemser, S. (1983). Learning to teach. In L. Shulman and G. Sykes, eds., *Handbook of teaching and policy.* New York: Longman.

Goodlad, J. (1986). *Toward a more perfect union.* Unpublished manuscript, University of Louisville, Louisville, KY.

Gowie, C. (1986). *Support for first-year teachers: New York State's mentor teacher-internship program.* Albany, NY: University of the State of New York and the State Education Department Office of ESC Education Planning and Support Services.

Grant, C. A.; and Zeichner, R. S. (1984). The socialization of beginning teachers through mentor-protege relationships. *Journal of Teacher Education, 35*(3), 21–24.

Hammond, L. D. (1984). *Beyond the commission reports: The coming crisis in teaching.* Santa Monica, CA: Rand.

Huling-Austin, L. (1985). Teacher induction programs: What is and isn't reasonable to expect. *R & DCTC Review, 3*(3). Austin, TX: The University of Texas at Austin, Research and Development Center for Teacher Education.

Lortie, D. C. (1966). Teacher socialization: The Robinson Crusoe model. In National Education Association, *The real world of the beginning teacher.* Washington, D.C.: NEA.

————(1975). *The school teacher.* Chicago:; University of Chicago Press.

Macdonald, F. (1980). The problems of beginning teachers: A crisis in training (vol. 1). In Educational Testing Service, *Study of induction programs for beginning teachers.* Princeton: Educational Testing Service.

New York State Legislative Commission on Rural Resources. (1985). *Rural New York in transition.* Albany, NY: State of New York.

Ryan, K., Newman, K. K., Mager, G., Applegate, J. H., Lasley, T., Flora, V. R., Johnson, J. (1980). *Biting the apple: Accounts of first year teachers.* New York: Longman.

Schlechty, P.; and Vance, V. (1983). Recruitment, selection and retention: The shape of the teaching force. *The Elementary School Journal, 83*(4), 469–487.

Sirotnik, K.; and Goodlad, J. (1988). *School-university partnerships in action: Concepts, cases, and concerns.* New York: Teachers College Press.

United States Office of Education. (1985). Partnership in education: Education trends of the future. Washington, D.C.: U.S.O.E.

Veenman, S. (1984). Perceived problems of beginning teachers. *Review of Educational Research, 54*(2), 143–178.

The Voice. (1989, October). *The Voice, 17*(2), 9.

Wolfe, M.; and Charland, J. (1989). Enhancing school climate: Capturing the spirit of university-school collaboration. *The Journal, 3*(12), 28–32.

5. The Arizona Teacher Residency Program:
Commitment, Collaboration, and Collegiality

BILLIE ENZ,
GARY W. ANDERSON,
BARBARA WEBER,
DON LAWHEAD

The Arizona Teacher Residency Program is described in this chapter by Enz, Anderson, Weber, and Lawhead. It reports the need for, practical aspects, and benefits of collaboration between colleges and universities and public schools for the enhanced professional development of teachers.

Commitment

The goal of this collaborative program is to provide immediate and ongoing instructional guidance and personal support to beginning teachers and teachers who are new to a district (residents). The program is based on the premise that teachers

    1. are a great source of talent and potential and deserve collegial support and the opportunity to exchange ideas and share information;

    2. want to increase their knowledge and skill and value the opportunity to increase their instructional effectiveness;

    3. welcome feedback from other teachers if it is structured, objective, and nonthreatening.

The underlying belief of the Arizona Teacher Residency Program (ATRP) is that beginning teachers who are provided support by a mentor—an effective, veteran teacher—will see a positive effect on their developing instructional skills. This development will, in turn, improve the quality of instruction their students receive.

97

Figure 5.1

ARIZONA TEACHER

RESIDENCY PROGRAM

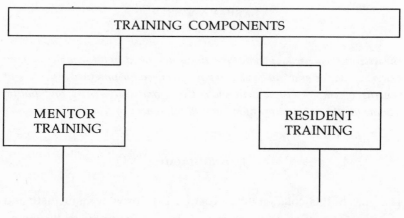

TRAINING COMPONENTS

MENTOR
TRAINING

RESIDENT
TRAINING

- Knowledge of thirty
  Competencies

- Skill Development in
  Observation, Scripting,
  Analysis

- Practice
  (Inter-Rater Reliability)

- Corresponding
  Instructional Strategies

- Conferencing

- Follow-Up Training

- Reliability Check

- Knowledge of thirty
  Competencies

- Practice in Observation,
  Scripting, Analysis

- Corresponding
  Instructional Strategies

- Follow-Up Training

Collaboration

A unique feature of the Arizona Teacher Residency Program (ATRP) involves the multiple perspectives and levels of interactions that have shaped the program's goals and delivery system. The term *resident* refers to beginning teachers, and the ATRP is an induction program developed for the support of beginning teachers. The ATRP is funded by the Arizona State Department of Education, and currently these funds are vested in two collaborative projects: the Center for Educational Development (CED) in Tucson and the Arizona State University/Maricopa County Teacher Training and Research Project (ASU) housed in the College of Education at Arizona State University.

As the service arm for the Pima County School System, CED specializes in providing in-service staff development programs to school districts in the southern portion of the state. The Center's primary responsibility for the ATRP includes program development, designing training materials, conducting local training, and the continued revision and enhancement of the program based on teacher input.

The ASU project is also responsible for training mentors and residents and for monitoring all phases of training. In addition, ASU studies beginning teacher performance and analyzes the factors that influence the mentor and resident relationship.

The cooperation and interaction between CED and ASU has been a critical factor in the evolution of a statewide program that has established consistent parameters for the role, responsibilities, and training of mentors, yet is responsive to the specific concerns of each of the twenty-four public school districts the program currently serves. One factor that has facilitated the program's implementation in school districts has been its adherence to the tenets of successful collaboration, which are critical to effective teacher education programs. These features have been defined by Griffin (1986) as purposeful and articulated, context sensitive, participatory, knowledge-based, ongoing, developmental, analytic, and reflective.

Briefly, the ATRP encourages both formal and informal interaction between mentors and residents. The formal requirements consist of a series of observation and conference sessions designed to confirm those things the resident does well and to target for improvement specific competencies that require additional work. The informal relationship consists of day-to-day instructional guidance and personal support. The rest of this chapter will detail the specifics of their interaction and describe the training that both mentors and residents attend.

The Arizona Teacher Residency Program (ATRP) is not mandated by the state but instead is an instructional improvement process in which schools choose to be involved. Once a district commits to participation, an action plan is developed that details the program requirements, clarifies expectations, and outlines financial obligations of the local district and the project providing these services. Through this process participating districts agree to maintain confidentiality and to separate the functions of instructional assessment and improvement from the formal evaluations process required by districts in personnel decisions. Research information is collected by the mentors and sent to project directors directly without being revealed to local school administrators.

Projects provide training materials, facilities, and a small stipend honorarium to mentors. Districts provide substitutes, identify mentors and resident teams, and are encouraged to support program activities through additional stipends or district credit. The most critical district responsibility is the selection of the mentors.

Who Shall Mentor?

Obviously the selection of the teacher who shall serve as mentor is critical to the success of any induction program. Based on criteria suggested by the program, mentors are identified by school building administrators. The guidelines for mentor characteristics include a teacher who (a) is established, effective, and acknowledged as such by peers (b) is a nurturing and supportive individual, (c) shares ideas and materials willingly but is also able to learn from the newcomer, (d) has time and is willing to mentor, and (e) can communicate easily and is able to describe the details of instructional methods and school policies and procedures as well. In addition, administrators must consider "team" factors that can affect the quality and quantity of communication, such as grade level and/or subject area match, and close physical proximity (next door, same wing).

Just as each school district is unique, so too is each school building within each district. Every school has its own culture and specific environmental concerns that can impact the resident's ability to succeed, that is, socioeconomic and ethnic diversity issues, community expectations, and so on. Therefore, it is highly recommended that residents are assigned to mentors who teach at the same school site. Mentors can then convey the intricacies of the schools' culture and help the residents cope with the environmental factors.

Lastly, another factor that may affect rapport is age difference. It appears that when a mentor is somewhat older than the resident, there is a greater chance that a positive rapport will evolve (Anderson & Enz 1990).

What Do Mentors Do?

As discussed previously, it is critical to the success of the program that the mentor establish a confidential, trusting relationship with the resident. Therefore, mentors in the Arizona Teacher Residency Program are *not* evaluators and do not participate in administrative decisions to either retain or release the beginning teacher. The ATRP mentor serves a complex dual role as professional, personal, and instructional advisor and clinical coach. In the role of professional advisor, the mentor provides support by informing the resident of district expectations, policies, procedures, and organizational structure. As a personal advisor, the mentor provides moral support and encouragement, friendship and acceptance. As instructional advisor, the mentor is a role model, demonstrating lessons and sharing instructional plans, materials and resources, classroom organization and management skills, and identifying effective discipline techniques.

Similarly, the mentor also serves as a clinical coach. In this role the mentor can directly influence the resident's instructional development through a continuous cycle of classroom observation, conferences, and feedback. By combining the responsibilities of clinical coach and advisor, and giving consistent, nonthreatening support, the mentor helps the resident enhance instructional and management skills.

Figure 5.2

COACHING

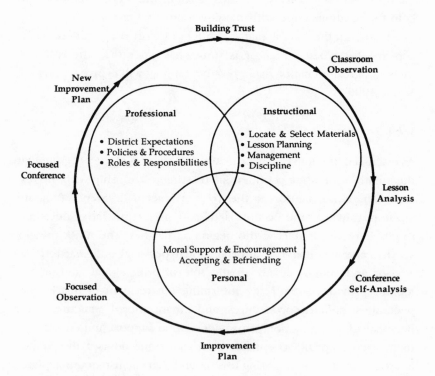

Components of Training: Assessment Instrument

To accomplish the goal of providing instructional guidance and personal support to residents, the program prepares established veteran teachers to mentor by providing training in assessment and clinical supervision. In addition, the program orients the residents to the goals and expectations of the ATRP and describes the mentor's responsibilities. This section will describe the training for new mentors and residents, and continuing mentors and residents.

Project directors from CED and ASU conduct an intensive sixteen-hour workshop for new mentor teachers. The training includes instruction in the use of an assessment instrument, observation and scripting skills, and conferencing and coaching techniques. Eight hours of the training involves instruction in the use of the Arizona Teacher Residency Instrument (Weber & Lawhead 1986) which helps the mentor objectively identify areas of instructional strength and concerns. The instrument includes thirty observable competencies in both hierarchical and discreet scale format and is divided into three sections:

1. *Teaching Plans and Materials.* This section of the instrument has seven competencies that assess the residents' ability to plan for instruction: (a) write instructional objectives, (b) identify teaching procedures, (c) assess and monitor student progress, and (d) plan for all levels of cognitive thinking and to provide for the wide range of student diversity in their classrooms.

2. *Classroom Procedures.* This section contains seventeen instructional competencies that assess the residents' ability to (a) use methods, media, and materials related to lesson objectives, (b) encourage student responses and to provide feedback, (c) use an anticipatory set and closure, (d) provide opportunities for student participation and involvement, (e) use classroom time effectively, and (f) attend to routine tasks.

3. *Interpersonal Skills.* This section of the instrument includes six competencies that assess the residents' ability to:(a) relate to and communicate with students, (b) motivate students through enthusiasm, warmth, and sensitivity, (c) positively reinforce student behavior, and (d) manage disruptive behavior.

During training the rationale for the inclusion of each competency and its relevance to the act of teaching is presented, and all indicators within each competency are thoroughly discussed. The following is an example of the discussion that accompanies the first competency in Teaching Plans and Materials, "Specifies Objectives for the Lesson."

As you know, a critical component of teaching is lesson planning. However, it is sometimes abbreviated by beginning teachers as they try to save themselves time. Unfortunately when they fail to mentally rehearse a lesson and document their thoughts they often overlook critical instructional consideration that can cause student confusion and teacher frustration. Remember, *P*roper *P*rior *P*lanning *P*revents *P*oor *P*erformance. Actually, lesson planning is a simple 3-step process:

1. What do you want students to be able to do at the end of the lesson?
2. How are you going to teach them? What resources and procedures will you use?
3. Do students know what you want them to know?

Competency 1 is "Specifies Objectives for the Lesson." If an instructional objective is well written, it will clearly communicate the teacher's intent as to what the students are to be able to do. The key to a good objective is the verb.

Examples: The student will be able to *write* the definition of the term secession.
Students will *list* one reason that the southern states wanted to secede from the union.

The entire lesson should be directed toward teaching students to perform the behavior described in the objective.

Figure 5.3

TEACHING PLANS AND MATERIALS

Directions: Mark one description which best applies to the lesson observed. If more information is needed, mark the appropriate "to clarify" box. Once this information is clarified, mark the one descriptor that best applies.

1. Specifies Objectives for the lesson

First Observation				Second Observation	
To clarify	Observed			To clarify	Observed
☐	☐	1.1	The instructional plans include no objectives.	1.1 ☐	☐
☐	☐	1.2	The plans include objectives which are written in broad non-measurable terms.	1.2 ☐	☐
☐	☐	1.3	The plans include objectives that with only a few exceptions are written in observable, measurable terms.	1.3 ☐	☐
☐	☐	1.4	All objectives are written in observable, measurable terms.	1.4 ☐	☐
☐	☐	1.5	In addition to the items included above, the objectives have been appropriately sequenced.	1.5 ☐	☐
☐	☐	1.6	Check this box only when the entire scale is determined inappropriate to the lesson observed. N/A	1.6 ☐	☐

Rationale: Rationale:

2. Specifies Teaching Procedures for Lesson

First Observation				Second Observation	
To clarify	Observed			To clarify	Observed
☐	☐	2.1	Plans do not specify teaching procedures.	2.1 ☐	☐
☐	☐	2.2	Teaching procedures are limited or are inappropriate for objectives.	2.2 ☐	☐
☐	☐	2.3	Teaching procedures are referenced to the objectives.	2.3 ☐	☐
☐	☐	2.4	All teaching procedures are appropriate for the objectives.	2.4 ☐	☐
☐	☐	2.5	In addition to the above, Plans specify procedures for both teacher-centered and student-centered approaches.	2.5 ☐	☐
☐	☐	2.6	Check this box only when the entire scale is determined inappropriate to the lesson observed. N/A	2.6 ☐	☐

Rationale: Rationale:

Figure 5.4

CLASSROOM PROCEDURES

Directions: Mark one description which best applies to the lesson observed. If more information is needed, mark the appropriate "to clarify" box. Once this information is clarified, mark the one descriptor that best applies.

1. Uses Instructional Equipment and Other Aids

First Observation				Second Observation	
To clarify	Observed			To clarify	Observed
☐	☐	1.1	Instructional equipment (e.g.projects) or appropriate aids (e.g., posters, charts) are not used when needed.	1.1 ☐	☐
☐	☐	1.2	Equipment or instructional aids are used but are not relevant to the objectives(s).	1.2 ☐	☐
☐	☐	1.3	Teacher effectively uses instructional equipment or other instructional aids at appropriate times in the lesson.	1.3 ☐	☐
☐	☐	1.4	Teacher is highly skillful in using instructional equipment or aids at appropriate times. Media blends smoothly with other kinds of instuction.	1.4 ☐	☐
☐	☐	1.5	In addition to the above, teacher uses original instructional aids which are relevant to the objective(s).	1.5 ☐	☐
☐	☐	1.6	Check this box only when the entire scale is determined inappropriate to the lesson observed. N/A	1.6 ☐	☐

Rationale:

Rationale:

2. Uses Instructional Materials To Encourage Appropriate Practice

First Observation				Second Observation	
To clarify	Observed			To clarify	Observed
☐	☐	2.1	Materials chosen are not relevant to topic or objectives or no materials are used when needed.	2.1 ☐	☐
☐	☐	2.2	Materials chosen are related to the topics being studied but not to the objective(s).	2.2 ☐	☐
☐	☐	2.3	Most materials chosen provide for practice on specific objectives. Practice may be insufficient in quantity to achieve the objective(s).	2.3 ☐	☐
☐	☐	2.4	Materials chosen are relevant to the objectives. Students are given ample opportunity to practice the objective(s).	2.4 ☐	☐
☐	☐	2.5	In addition to the above, progress assessment techniques are used to determine whether the practice individual students receive is sufficient.	2.5 ☐	☐
☐	☐	2.6	Check this box only when the entire scale is determined inappropriate to the lesson observed. N/A	2.6 ☐	☐

Rationale:

Rationale:

Figure 5.5

INTERPERSONAL SKILLS

Directions: Mark one description which best applies to the lesson observed. If more information is needed, mark the appropriate "to clarify" box. Once this information is clarified, mark the one descriptor that best applies.

1. Communicates Enthusiasm

First Observation			Second Observation
☐	1.1 None	1.1	☐
☐	1.2 One	1.2	☐
☐	1.3 Two	of the descriptors are evident	1.3	☐
☐	1.4 Three	1.4	☐
☐	1.5 Four	Check this box only when the entire scale is	1.5	☐
☐	1.6 N/A	determined inappropriate to the lesson observed. N/A	1.6	☐

To clarify	Observed			To clarify	Observed
☐	☐	a	Eye contact or facial expressions communicate pleasure, concern, interest, etc.	a ☐	☐
☐	☐	b	Voice inflections stress points of interest and importance	b ☐	☐
☐	☐	c	Posture (moving around room or sitting among students) communicates enthusiasm.	c ☐	☐
☐	☐	d	Gestures to accentuate points; communicates enthusiasm	d ☐	☐

Rationale: Rationale:

2. Demonstrates Warmth and Friendliness

First Observation			Second Observation
☐	2.1 None	2.1	☐
☐	2.2 One	of the descriptors are evident	2.2	☐
☐	2.3 Two	2.3	☐
☐	2.4 Three	2.4	☐
☐	2.5 Four	Check this box only when the entire scale is	2.5	☐
☐	2.6 N/A	determined inappropriate to the lesson observed. N/A	2.6	☐

To clarify	Observed			To clarify	Observed
☐	☐	a	Teacher asks about students' interests and opinions.	a ☐	☐
☐	☐	b	Teacher smiles at students or laughs or jokes with them.	b ☐	☐
☐	☐	c	Teacher sits or stands near students.	c ☐	☐
☐	☐	d	Teacher uses students' name in a warm and friendly way.	d ☐	☐

Rationale: Rationale:

Figure 5.6

The Thirty Competencies on the Arizona Teacher Residency Instrument

Teaching Plans and Materials (TPM)

TPM	#1	Specifies objectives for the lesson.
TPM	#2	Specifies teaching procedures for the lesson.
TPM	#3	Specifies resources for the lesson.
TPM	#4	Specifies procedures for assessing student progress.
TPM	#5	Plans for all levels of cognitive thinking.
TPM	#6	Plans for variety of student abilities and styles.
TPM	#7	Plans include monitoring student progress and providing feedback.

Classroom Procedures (CP)

CP	#1	Uses instructional equipment and other aids.
CP	#2	Uses instructional materials to encourage appropriate practice.
CP	#3	Gives directions and explanations related to lesson.
CP	#4	Presents information which relates directly to the objective.
CP	#5	Uses student responses and questions in teaching.
CP	#6	Provides student feedback throughout lesson.
CP	#7	Uses a variety of teaching methods appropriately and effectively.
CP	#8	Demonstrates ability to work with individuals, small groups, and large groups.
CP	#9	Focuses student attention early in lesson.
CP	#10	Provides opportunities for participation.
CP	#11	Maintains student involvement.
CP	#12	Provides opportunity for closure or summarization.
CP	#13	Provides instruction which promotes students' retention.
CP	#14	Demonstrates knowledge in subject area.
CP	#15	Attends to routine tasks.
CP	#16	Uses instructional time effectively.
CP	#17	Maintains an attractive and stimulating learning environment.

Interpersonal Skills (IS)

IS	#1	Communicates enthusiasm.
IS	#2	Demonstrates warmth and friendliness.
IS	#3	Is sensitive to needs and feelings of students.
IS	#4	Provides feedback to students about behavior.
IS	#5	Maintains positive classroom behavior.
IS	#6	Manages disruptive behavior.

When objectives are measurable, as described above, the teacher is able to stop at significant points in the lesson and check to see which of the students are able to perform correctly, and those who need additional instruction.

Let's look at the indicators in Competency 1.

1.1 No objectives are included in the lesson

The lesson plan doesn't include any objectives.

1.2 Objectives are not written in measurable terms

Objectives such as "student will know/understand/appreciate" are hard to measure. How will the teacher be able to detect what the students have actually learned?

1.3 to 1.4 All of the objectives are written in measurable terms

1.5 In addition to being written in measurable terms, the objectives are sequenced in a logical order

The teacher determined the lesson sequence that would provide success for the students in her class (Weber 1987, 1989).

After the seven competencies in Teaching Plans and Materials have been reviewed, mentors use the assessment instrument to evaluate a set of lesson plans. To increase objectivity and specificity, the mentors must provide a written rationale to justify each numerical rating. Then, in triads, mentors compare individual ratings and arrive at a consensus rating for these competencies. Finally, the triad consensus is reported to the entire group. To begin to establish inter-rater reliability, triad ratings are compared to one another and finally compared to the panel of expert's assessment.

After the seventeen competencies in Classroom Procedures and the six competencies in Interpersonal Skills are presented, mentors are taught to script. Observing, recording, and assessing the residents' actual teaching performance is an important aspect of mentoring, and scripting enables the mentors to record the resident's classroom performance and allows for a detailed analysis of the lesson. To practice this skill, mentors observe and script a twenty-minute videotape of an actual classroom lesson. After viewing the lesson, mentors individually clarify, amplify, and analyze their script notes and assess the lesson using the competencies in the Classroom Procedures and

Interpersonal Skills sections. Again, after individual analysis the mentors work in triads to reach rating consensus. The triads con- -sensus is again reported and compared to others and to the experts'. Mentor teachers report that the "individual-to-small group" process promotes self-analysis by providing an objective method to examine and assess their own lesson plans and teaching skills (Enz & Anderson 1989).

In addition to mentor training, the Arizona Teacher Residency Program believes it is essential to provide training to the residents. Residents attend an eight-hour orientation similar to the first day of the mentor training. This orientation decreases anxiety residents may have regarding assessment and provides an understanding of what they can expect a mentor to do. By completing the same training with the assessment instrument, residents come to share a common vocabulary of instructional terminology with their mentor. This shared language and shared expectations facilitates mentor/resident communication.

New mentor and resident training focuses on three major program objectives: first, it brings the art and science of teaching to the conscious level; second, it labels and defines effective instructional strategies; and third, within a structure targeted at instructional improvement, it establishes a foundation for the relationship between mentor and resident.

Collegiality

Components of Training: Coaching and Conferencing

Conferencing is an important aspect of mentoring because it is when coaching begins. During the postobservation conference, the resident and mentor identify areas of strength and concern and work together to develop an instructional improvement plan. During the second day of training, mentors are taught some of the art and skill of coaching. To ensure the successful rapport and communication between mentors and residents, mentors work in groups to brainstorm words that describe a successful "coaching environment." In addition, mentors learn, through role-play, how subtle nonverbal skills such as posture, facial expressions, eye contact, physical space, and body positioning can affect interpersonal relationships and either impede or facilitate communication.

Mentors also practice the verbal skills necessary to encourage the residents to reflect on their lessons. Such techniques as open and closed-ended questions, paraphrasing, positive phrasing, and empathy statements are explained and then rehearsed. Finally, mentors are taught to use a five-step conference format (Weber 1989) that is structured to increase the opportunity for resident input and involvement. The five steps of the conference are described below.

Positive feeling tone. A positive statement, made by the mentor about the lesson, decreases possible tension and increases the likelihood of an effective conference.

Reviewing the steps of the conference. The mentor outlines the conference format and informs the resident about their active role in it.

Resident input. Residents are asked to review their lesson and identify what they felt contributed to student learning (reinforcement), and what they would do differently if reteaching the same lesson to the same students (refinement). Residents often need encouragement and guidance to reflect and analyze their own instructional performance.

Mentor input.

From the analysis of the lesson plan, observation and script notes and subsequent rating on the instrument, the mentor has selected one competency from all thirty to reinforce and one to refine (improve).

(a) Reinforcement. A competency that was demonstrated to a degree of proficiency and has the greatest impact on student learning is selected for reinforcement. The mentor identifies and labels the skill, lists the benefits of this skill to students and to the teacher, relates how that competency effects other areas of instruction and encourages the resident to use this skill in other content areas, lessons, and circumstances.

(b) Refinement. The mentor identifies a competency in need of improvement. It is critical to the continued success of the mentor/resident team for the resident to have a positive experience when attempting to improve instruction. Therefore, the mentor selects *only one* competency from the thirty to refine. The selection of this area of refinement is based on several criteria:

1. *What will make the most significant difference to student learning?* Which skill/technique will contribute most to student learning?

2. *Are some skills dependent upon others?* In order for a teacher to understand and implement the concept of monitoring and adjusting, the resident must first understand and use techniques of active participation.

3. *What is known about the teacher?* Is the resident shy? Insecure? What has worked in the past? Not worked? Are there discipline problems? Problems with parents or administrators?

4. *What does the mentor understand well enough to teach?* Unless the mentor thoroughly understand and uses the skill, no attempt should be made to teach it to another.

5. *What is the smallest guaranteed win?* Mentors should make sure that the advice they offer is going to be immediately successful for the resident. This will create greater confidence in the mentor's ability to help, and encourage the resident to trust the mentor's expertise and experience.

Coaching skills are perhaps most utilized at the moment the mentor begins to identify the area targeted for refinement (improvement). When possible, the goal of the mentor is to conduct a conference that addresses self-identified needs of the resident while simultaneously targeting the concern identified by the mentor. The mentor should be able to help the resident leave the conference feeling they did a good job in self-analysis and that self-perceived needs were met.

However, beginning teachers may perceive only the surface symptoms of a larger problem. For example, the resident feels the students were restless and the resident needs to improve discipline techniques. Restless students may indeed have been a problem, but students restlessness may just be a symptom that the lesson needed to include more opportunities for active student participation. The mentor's job in the conference is to link these two factors as cause and effect and help the resident see the connection between active involvement and increased on-task student behavior. In addition, it is important for the resident to understand that when students are actively involved they are on-task, consequently learn more, are less likely to be restless, and the teacher doesn't need to reteach as often or discipline as much.

The mentor must introduce the skill to be refined and teach it to the resident just as one would to students in the classroom. The mentors are asked to establish a purpose for learning the skill to be refined, provide all pertinent information about the skill, model the skill, and then check the resident's understanding by allowing the resident a chance to mentally rehearse and verbally practice the new skill.

Closure.

The last step of the conference provides the resident the opportunity to cement new learning. Closure provides the chance for the resident to summarize the coaching that was initiated by the mentor. A mentor might ask, "Focusing on concepts, what did we discuss today that increased the students' opportunity for . . ." In addition, closure provides an opportunity for the mentor to monitor the resident's understanding of the concepts and strategies discussed in both the areas of reinforcement and refinement.

Focused Observations and Conference

At the end of the conference the mentor and resident establish a time for the mentor to revisit the resident's classroom and complete a focused observation. The focused observation concentrates on how well the resident has progressed in implementing the area of refinement. The focused observation is then followed by the focused conference. At that time, a new area of refinement may be identified and the coaching cycle continues.

The Arizona Teacher Residency Program requires that the mentors make one full observation/conference and one focused observation/conference in the fall. They then repeat this pattern in the spring. After each full observation, the mentors send in the Observation Summary Sheet (a record of the performance level on each of the thirty competencies) to the ASU Project. This information is summarized within and across districts to provide specific staff development information about beginning teacher needs.

Components of Training: Continuing Mentors

In addition to providing an opportunity to review and practice scripting and lesson analysis skills, the continuing mentor workshop offers training in four alternative observation methods. These methods are highly specific and may be used to collect data to "pinpoint" problems for the focused observations. Which technique is used depends on the type of information that would be most meaningful to the resident. The purpose of all these techniques is to provide the mentor and resident enough objective information to begin to resolve most of the resident's instructional concerns. The observation methods are selective verbatim, verbal flow, at-task behavior charting, and class traffic. Once this new information is presented it is immediately followed with an opportunity to practice the new skill.

Selective verbatim. The mentor acts as an auditory sorter, recording only a specific category of statements identified as areas of concern by the resident. For example, if the resident is concerned about their questioning skills, the mentor will record only the questions the teacher asks. Mentor and resident then review the selective script to determine the quality of questions, frequency, and so on.

Verbal flow. A verbal flow chart is one way to determine how the resident inhibits or encourages student participation in classroom-

Figure 5.7

. Summary Sheet .

Resident Name _____ Date _____

Mentor Name _____ Date _____

District _____

Observation Number

1	2

Directions: Using your completed instrument, please transpose your response for each scale item by placing an X in the correct box.

TEACHING PLANS & MATERIALS						
(1)	(2)	(3)	(4)	(5)	(6)	(7)
1.1	2.1	3.1	4.1	5.1	6.1	7.1
1.2	2.2	3.2	4.2	5.2	6.2	7.2
1.3	2.3	3.3	4.3	5.3	6.3	7.3
1.4	2.4	3.4	4.4	5.4	6.4	7.4
1.5	2.5	3.5	4.5	5.5	6.5	7.5
1.6	2.6	3.6	4.6	5.6	6.6	7.6

CLASSROOM PROCEDURES																
(1)	(2)	(3)	(4)	(5)	(6)	(7)	(8)	(9)	(10)	(11)	(12)	(13)	(14)	(15)	(16)	(17)
1.1	2.1	3.1	4.1	5.1	6.1	7.1	8.1	9.1	10.1	11.1	12.1	13.1	14.1	15.1	16.1	17.1
1.2	2.2	3.2	4.2	5.2	6.2	7.2	8.2	9.2	10.2	11.2	12.2	13.2	14.2	15.2	16.2	17.2
1.3	2.3	3.3	4.3	5.3	6.3	7.3	8.3	9.3	10.3	11.3	12.3	13.3	14.3	15.3	16.3	17.3
1.4	2.4	3.4	4.4	5.4	6.4	7.4	8.4	9.4	10.4	11.4	12.4	13.4	14.4	15.4	16.4	17.4
1.5	2.5	3.5	4.5	5.5	6.5	7.5	8.5	9.5	10.5	11.5	12.5	13.5	14.5	15.5	16.5	17.5
1.6	2.6	3.6	4.6	5.6	6.6	7.6	8.6	9.6	10.6	11.6	12.6	13.6	14.6	15.6	16.6	17.6

INTERPERSONAL SKILLS					
(1)	(2)	(3)	(4)	(5)	(6)
1.1	2.1	3.1	4.1	5.1	6.1
1.2	2.2	3.2	4.2	5.2	6.2
1.3	2.3	3.3	4.3	5.3	6.3
1.4	2.4	3.4	4.4	5.4	6.4
1.5	2.5	3.5	4.5	5.5	6.5
1.6	2.6	3.6	4.6	5.6	6.6

1. CONFERENCE REINFORCEMENT

_____

(EXAMPLE TPM 1)

2. CONFERENCE REFINEMENT

_____

(EXAMPLE CP 12)

SUMMARIZE INSTRUCTIONAL IMPROVEMENT STRATEGIES TO BE
IMPLEMENTED BY THE RESIDENT TEACHER

_____

_____

_____

discussions. The mentor uses a seating chart and draws arrows to track the verbal interactions between teacher and students and student to student. This type of tracking can also be used to determine if there is any type of teacher bias simply by identifying the gender, ethnicity, or ability level of the students after the original information is collected.

At-task behavior charting. At-task behavior is a variable that correlates strongly with student achievement. At-task observations provide data that indicate whether or not individual students are engaged in the tasks the teacher has established as appropriate. Many teachers are surprised when they see, recorded on paper, the number of students who were overtly off-task—without the teacher being aware that the behavior was taking place.

Class traffic. Class traffic is used to determine classroom organization and management. This observation technique uses a diagram of the arrangement of the classroom and includes a student seating chart. The mentor tracks the physical movement of the teacher and/or students, depending on the resident's concerns.

Components of Training: Continuing Residents

The participating districts may elect to have residents continue a second or third year with their mentor. Such residents complete an additional day of training to improve their professional efficiency and to make more effective use of instructional time. Research from the Beginning Teacher Evaluation Study (BTES) (Fisher et al. 1980) indicates that less effective teachers spend as much as 40 to 60 percent of any school day in noninstructional activities (routine tasks, changing activities, etc.). In direct contrast, the BTES found that the most effective teachers used 85 percent or more of the school day in instructional concerns. These effective teachers have highly streamlined routines established in their classrooms and focus their teaching time on students and instruction. The information presented during this eight-hour training includes:

1. *Planning routine tasks.* Attendance, lunch counts, permission slips, early arriver activities, think pads, signal and transitions, pencil sharpening and supply distribution, toileting procedures, and early finishers.

2. *Advanced routine tasks.* Grading systems, drinking fountain and line waiting activities, classroom helpers, assignment calendars, study buddy, traffic patterns, and sponge activities.

3. *Teaching routine tasks.* When to teach, how to teach, how to reinforce new skills.

4. *Giving directions.* Rules for direction giving, timing, sequencing, chunking, and signals.

5. *Positive feeling tone.* Teaching for student success, nonverbal cues, the Law of Least Intervention, selective inattention, and effective rewards for positive behavior.

All training, whether for new or continuing mentors and residents, emphasizes the developmental nature of the teaching profession and encourages all participants to engage in collegial networking. This program is designed to make the tradition of isolationalism and the norm of noninterference a relic of the past. The health of our professional present and future may well depend upon the potential of induction programs such as the ATRP.

Research, Response, and Reflection

Griffin (1986) suggests that important features of effective educational programs and successful collaboration include analysis and reflection. The Arizona Teacher Residency Program through the Arizona State University Project strives to maintain a variety of research activities that assess (a) the effectiveness of training, (b) the residents' initial instructional performance and subsequent improvement, (c) mentors' and residents' satisfaction with their formal and personal relationship, (d) residents' and mentors' perceptions of mentor functions, and (e) the frequency, purpose, and duration of communication between mentors and residents.

These activities, supported with the qualitative data of mentor and resident teachers' suggestions that are collected by both Center for Educational Development and ASU, are part of an evolving research agenda designed to provide feedback to the projects for training modification, to provide specific staff development information to participating school districts, and to add to the knowledge base of beginning teacher performance and induction programs.

References

Anderson, G. W.; and Enz, B. J. (1990). When mentors and beginners talk: What are the issues? Paper presented at the annual Association of Supervision and Curriculum Development, San Antonio, TX.

Enz, B. J.; and Anderson, G. W. (1989). Instruction in assessment and supervision: Effects on mentor and residents' classroom performance. Paper presented at the annual meeting for the Association of Teacher Educators, St. Louis, MO.

Fisher, C. W.; Berliner, D. C., Filby, N. N., Marliave, R., Cohen, L. S., & Dishaw, M. M. (1980). Teaching behaviors, academic learning time, and student achievement: An overview. In C. Denham and A. Lieberman, eds., *Time to learn.* Washington, DC: National Institute of Education.

Griffin, G. (1986). Clinical Teacher Education. In J. Hoffman and S. Edwards, eds., *Reality and reform in clinical teacher education.* New York: Random House.

Weber, B. (1987). *Arizona teacher residency program resource handbook.* Phoenix, AZ: Arizona State Department of Education.

————. (1989). *Arizona teacher residency program trainers manual.* Phoenix, AZ: Arizona State Department of Education.

Weber, B.; and Lawhead, D. (1986). *The Arizona teacher residency instrument.* Phoenix, AZ: Arizona State Department of Education.

6. Collaborative Relationships in a Mentoring Program in East Harlem Schools

CHRISTINA TAHARALLY,
MAE GAMBLE,
SUSAN MARSA

Taharally, Gamble, and Marsa describe a collaborative effort by a public school and Hunter College to provide specific support for minority teachers in Community School District Four in East Harlem, Manhattan. Funding, objectives, training, interaction, and positive results are reported. The urban setting and specific goal of supporting minority teachers may be of special interest in this chapter.

Introduction and Background

Every major report published in the past decade underscores the fact that public education is facing serious crises. One problem is the recruitment and retention of minority teachers, especially in inner-city environments where their presence as role models is seriously needed. Unfortunately, many minority teachers who enter teaching drop out within the first five years (New York Times 1988). Each year as much as 40 percent of the new teacher population in the New York City schools leave the profession (Pflaum & Abramson 1989). Teaching in urban schools can be a daunting task, and some studies report that as many as 60 percent of all teachers nationally drop out of teaching within the first five years (Tikunoff & Ward 1987; Darling-Hammond 1984).

The problem of retention of minority teachers is particularly worrisome in New York City, where approximately 78 percent of the school-age population is of minority background. Haberman (1988) states that the disparity between increasing enrollment of African-American and Hispanic children and the corresponding drop in the number of minority teachers points to a worsening of the problems of

·educating minority children and youth in inadequate elementary and secondary schools.

Other empirical studies suggest that beginning teachers in inner-city schools need the help and support of their school district personnel, principals, and experienced teachers in order to survive the initial difficulties encountered in the first year (Veenman 1984, Odell 1986, Huffman & Leak 1986). Support teams that include mentors or college personnel have often been able to provide the assistance needed to help beginning teachers deal with first-year difficulties (Shulman 1986). Schwartz (1989) suggests that models of collaboration within school districts can create the kind of situation that enhances teachers' performance and leadership.

Hunter College of the City University of New York, with the assistance of a Teacher Opportunity Corps Grant from the New York State Education Department and a supplemental grant from the Aaron Diamond Foundation, sought to create a collaboration with Community School District Four in East Harlem. The result was a program to mentor beginning minority teachers and support them in their first three years of teaching. It involved college personnel, the District Administration, and twenty-one public schools in East Harlem in a special collaborative relationship over the past three years. This chapter describes the process of establishing and maintaining the collaborative relationships that developed and assesses the benefits that accrued as college and school district personnel worked with principals and master teachers in this mentoring program.

Need and Purpose

For the past twenty years, Hunter College of the City University of New York has enjoyed a collaborative relationship with Community School District Four in East Harlem, Manhattan. Since 1970, under-graduate field-based education programs for training preservice teachers for inner-city schools were supported by the district. Under-graduates often obtain jobs in those schools in which they did their student teaching. After repeated requests for advice and support from beginning teachers, it became clear that completion of the undergraduate degree was only a first step toward becoming a competent teacher. These teachers needed additional support and training. Many appeared ready to quit teaching when they realized that their schools were not compatible with their developing educational philosophies and teaching styles. Several others reported feeling that they lacked the skills to survive in the hostile environment they experienced, and a few left because of their inability to get along with building principals. The first year of full-time teaching was particularly traumatic. If a major goal was retention of teachers in the city schools, a program to support them in their development from novice to capable professionals appeared to be a necessity.

Funding and Objectives

With funding provided by a grant from the New York State Education Department, the Teacher Opportunity Corps was established in 1987. The overriding goal was the development of a collaborative relationship between Hunter College and Community School District Four that would support teachers in the inner-city schools and retain more teachers from minority groups historically underrepresented in the New York City Public Schools. The following specific objectives were adapted from goals articulated by Ward and Tikunoff (1987):

1. Provision of academic and personal-social support that was not available from other sources to thirty new minority teachers in the East Harlem schools each year.

2. Development of greater understanding in participating institutions (Hunter College and Community School District Four) of the needs of beginning teachers in inner-city schools.

3. Increase in the number of minority teachers, especially African-Americans and Hispanics among the teaching ranks by the following means: (a) maintaining new teachers'

enthusiasm for and commitment to teaching, (b) reducing new teachers' sense of isolation, (c) helping new and prospective teachers to prepare for the NTE and NYC Board of Education tests and obtain the necessary licenses, (d) assisting new teachers in finding situations that are congruent with their teaching philosophy and personality.

Program Implementation

With the exception of minor modifications, the collaborative mentoring program remained basically stable over three years. In June of each year, Teacher Opportunity Corps (TOC) staff visited principals from District Four schools to discuss anticipated vacancies. Graduates of Hunter College's undergraduate programs in teacher education were notified of the anticipated openings, the culture of the school, its philosophy, and the principal's expectations.

In September, new teachers in the district were informed of Hunter College's Teacher Opportunity Corps (TOC) Program and invited to apply. Approximately thirty beginning teachers were admitted each year, about half of whom were graduates of Teacher Education Programs at Hunter College. As soon as the new teachers were identified, notices went out to experienced teachers in the same schools advertising a vacancy for mentor teachers to work with these beginning teachers. Mentors were expected to have at least five years of outstanding teaching experience at a specific level such as Early Childhood or Middle Grades, appropriate educational degrees, and familiarity with a variety of teaching styles and methodologies. Good human relations skills and a willingness to meet with the new teacher one day a week after school were also necessary.

Prospective mentors applied directly or were nominated by building principals. Nominations and applications were reviewed by a committee made up of the building principal, the United Federation of Teachers chapter chairperson, the director of communication arts, and the Hunter College TOC director. The committee discussed each application and selected mentors based on qualifications and needs. Mentor teachers were then assigned one or two new teachers whom they supported and trained during the academic year. We shall refer to these beginning teachers as "interns."

The mentoring program started in October and continued to June. Each mentor was paid for using one preparation period per week to visit each new teacher in his or her classroom. Mentors were also paid at a per-session rate for meeting with interns after school and for attending mentor workshops. The after-school sessions with interns focused on what the mentor observed while visiting and on determining solutions to problems that the intern was experiencing. Mentor workshops were held monthly and were designed to refine mentoring skills. The topics of these workshops were as follows: building trust, understanding the role of the mentor, identifying and solving problems, developing communication skills, and offering constructive criticism.

The two professors who were assigned to fieldwork also met with the mentors regularly to discuss the interns' progress and coordinate suggestions to be given to interns. At these meetings, strategies for dealing with the interns' needs were identified and priorities were established. The mentors offered to do demonstration lessons or scheduled specific observation sessions with the intern. If a schedule change was necessary, an administrator was usually willing to assist. Care was taken not to overburden the intern but to pace demands and encourage growth. Often there was complete agreement among professors and mentors on the analysis of strengths and weaknesses of the interns and possible strategies to use. Mentors' sessions with interns might include topics such as the following: dealing with disruptive children, handling transitions, writing lesson plans, getting along with administrators, and communicating with parents.

Interns also made interclass visits using at least one preparation period per week. The interns' observations took place either in the mentor's classroom or that of another experienced teacher. Interns earned six college credits per year for working with mentors. These credits were applied toward the Master of Science in Elementary Education degree offered by Hunter College.

Interns also earned six college credits by taking two required courses offered to new TOC participants in the Hunter College Master's Degree Program. One course, The Art of Teaching, was taught by a Hunter College professor; the other, Teaching Reading and the Language Arts in the Elementary School, was taught by an adjunct professor and former staff developer in the district. The professors spent two or three days per week in the school district, visiting the interns and conferring with the mentors and district personnel. Because of this kind of involvement, professors were able to relate the content of courses directly to the classroom experiences of interns. When they felt it would be helpful, professors also modeled effective teaching through direct work with children.

Interns who completed the first year of the mentoring program continued in the second year to take courses each semester to fulfill requirements of the master's degree program. They attended classes at Hunter College and met other beginning teachers from throughout the metropolitan area. The two Hunter College professors also continued to visit and offer support to second- or third-year TOC participants whenever they were in their schools. Second- and third-year participants also benefited from special seminars and visits arranged by TOC staff and paid for from project funds.

Important Components of the Collaborative Relationship

The successful establishment and implementation of the Mentoring Program was possible in part because of a history of collaboration and trust that existed between the district and the faculty involved in the program. The project director enjoyed a twenty-year working relationship with personnel in the school district, as did the two professors who taught TOC participants and visited schools.

Communication among all groups was treated with extreme care in this program. Project personnel ensured that schedules of visits were shared and that principals and district staff were always aware of what activities were planned.

Principals trusted the college staff, and interns and mentors soon learned that all discussions were considered confidential. Project personnel also emphasized that interns were to be helped, not judged. Over time, the interns came to regard both school and college personnel as allies rather than supervisors. This element of trust was important in facilitating the smooth implementation and development of the program.

Principals, mentors, and college personnel also shared a sense of responsibility for the intern. This had a positive impact on the school as a whole. The idea of shared responsibility was especially important at this time because many schools in New York City were beginning to move toward "school-based management and shared decision making."

Another key aspect of the collaborative relationship was a cooperative approach to teacher placement. TOC Project staff tried to ensure that there was a good match between the intern and the school. If it became apparent during the year that the philosophy of the school was incompatible with the intern's developing style, the college and district personnel tried to find a more appropriate placement. Four interns were moved to schools that were better suited to their particular strengths. If they had remained in their first assignments, they might have left teaching.

Generally, the collaborative relationships were characterized by respect, collegiality, and willingness to do whatever was necessary to recruit and retain qualified teachers in the East Harlem schools. Advisory committee meetings allowed other constituents such as parents and even state legislators to propose ways in which they could be involved in the maintenance of the mentoring program. These factors appear to have had an impact on the 98 percent retention rate of new teachers in the program over the past three years. Seventy-eight percent of these teachers are of minority background. This is a remarkable achievement, as the national retention rate for minority teachers

Figure 6.1

Model of Relationships in the TOC Program

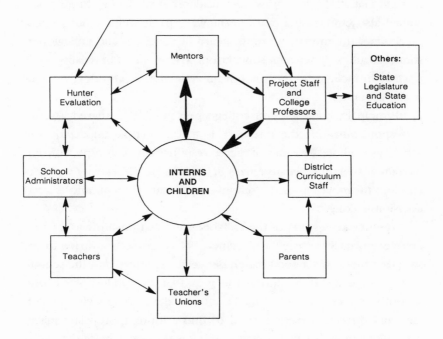

has been abysmally low and is expected to drop even lower by the turn of the century.

Figure 6.1 illustrates the strength of the collaborations that exist among the groups involved. The thickness of the arrows indicates the frequency and depth of interactions. The model of relationships that has evolved works very well. There has been little modification of the program as a whole except to intensify documentation and evaluation efforts.

This program viewed mentoring as a process that enabled the socialization of the new teacher into the culture of teaching and classroom life. Mentors were seen as "master-teachers who guided beginning teachers into their new role" (Yarger-Kane & Buck 1989).

The specific approach to mentoring that grew out of this program seemed to be of the initiator model reflected in the work of Huling-Austin (1990), in which she states that "initiators believe it is their responsibility to facilitate the professional growth of the beginning teacher to the greatest degree possible." TOC staff believed this approach was the most effective because it helped interns quickly gain skills in classroom management and curriculum planning. These were two areas in which new teachers appeared to need the most help, as shown by an analysis of professor's logs in our own evaluation and in the work of Odell (1991).

Evaluation

The evaluation of the program may be described as organic in nature. It grew as project staff sought to document the evolution and development of the program. Data on the perceptions of principals, mentors, and interns were gathered, and these provide insight into the processes that occurred and their impact on individuals.

Analysis of Logs

College personnel realized very early in the program that there was a need to document what was occurring. In the first year, information was collected mainly to satisfy funding requirements. Simple questionnaires were constructed and administered to find out areas of success or concern. However, one of the professors who taught a course and visited interns in their rooms kept a log of meetings during the first four semesters of the program. On each visit, an intern was observed for at least one class period. The professor kept a running record of that period and of the postobservation conference. Often a meeting with the mentor of that intern was also held and the details recorded. A content analysis was made of the logs and occurrences of incidents, and events were categorized under the headings of coordination, assessment of needs, suggestions for curriculum, suggestions for management, and positive coaching. Positive coaching is defined as "catching and highlighting the positive things the new teacher intentionally or accidentally does while teaching the children in her classroom." Table 6.1 shows the number of times a professor needed to give attention to a particular event. Each event is recorded as a raw score and as a percentage of total time required for that activity during the school year. The areas of curriculum improvement, classroom management, and positive coaching required the most time as shown by table 6.1. These results are consistent with other studies that cited the two most frequently identified needs of new teachers as being those of support in the instructional process and management of children (Odell 1991).

Development of Mentor Questionnaires

To understand better the dynamics of the mentor-intern relationship, two open-ended questionnaires were given to mentors in the second year of the project, one at the end of the first semester and the other at the end of the second semester. The aim of the first questionnaire was to determine what aspects of the mentoring process seemed to be successful. Mentors described the most successful or least successful aspects of mentor workshops and made suggestions for changes in workshop sessions. Some of the positive aspects of mentoring identified by mentors were "doing demonstration workshops, seeing interns grow in confidence, and getting flexibility in scheduling." These and other descriptive statements on aspects of the mentoring process

Table 6.1
*Analysis of Professor's Logs**

Activity	Year 1	%	Year 2	%
Coordination	15	8.5	22	8.4
Assessment of Needs	8	4.7	24	9.5
Curriculum Suggestions	56	31.9	95	34.4
Management Suggestions	150	94.7	244	90.9
Positive Coaching	94	34.3	151	55.9

*Reported as raw scores and as percentages of professor's time on each activity

were used to construct rating scales in the third year of the program. The results of these rating scales are presented later in this chapter.

The aim of the second questionnaire was to determine the characteristics of the relationships between mentors and interns. The questionnaire consisted of nine questions that asked mentors to do the following: characterize their initial relationship with the intern; describe the personal and professional changes in the intern; assess their own personal and professional growth; assess the impact of their mentoring role on prior relationships with principals and coworkers; and assess the human-relations aspect of the mentoring relationship. Mentors described interns as friendly and cooperative or enthusiastic or frustrated at different times. In another section, mentors reported that interns became more comfortable in the relationship, more receptive to suggestions, and less defensive. These descriptive statements were incorporated into the mentor rating scale used in the third year of the program.

Development of the Intern Questionnaire

The aim of the intern questionnaire was to determine how interns perceived various aspects of the mentoring relationship. Interns' responses on help received in curriculum planning indicated that mentors reviewed units, discussed plans and resources available, suggested ideas for grouping in reading, and generally helped to plan for different curriculum areas. In describing their relationship with the mentor, interns reported that they felt comfortable and were not embarrassed when talking with their mentor. They liked having someone on whom to depend. They reported less anxiety and more feelings of competence and security in their jobs. These and similar statements were used to construct an intern rating scale, the results of which are presented later.

Development of Principal Questionnaire

At the conclusion of the second year, principals also responded to a ten-item questionnaire. The aim of this questionnaire was to find out whether principals observed any personal and professional changes in mentors and interns as a result of the mentoring process. The summary statements provided principals' perceptions on various aspects of personal and professional growth of mentors and interns. Principals reported that mentors appeared to demonstrate more leadership skills, better understanding of new teachers' problems, and more tolerance and patience generally. Principals also noted that there was greater willingness among teachers to assist one another. They felt that the mentoring program provided an opportunity for teachers to view themselves as helpers of newcomers, and it reinforced the belief that teachers learn best from peers.

Results of Rating Scales

Mentors' Ratings

In the third year of the program, mentors responded to a rating scale consisting of items that reflected their answers in previous open-ended questionnaires. Table 6.2 shows samples of mentors' ratings of various aspects of the mentoring experience. When asked to judge the effectiveness of workshops that they attended, mentors reported that several workshops were successful in extending their knowledge greatly or moderately. The most effective workshops are listed in section (i) of table 6.2. In section (ii) of the table, *Mentors' Perception of the Degree of Help needed by Interns,* it is reported that mentors perceived interns to be more competent in coordinating class activities and assessing the needs of children. Mentors reported that curriculum suggestions, management suggestions, and positive coaching were the areas in which interns needed the most help. These reports are consistent with the observations made in the analysis of logs earlier. This is reasonable as those are areas in which new teachers gain competence only through practice.

The third section of table 6.2 recounts mentors' reflections on their own growth. They mention feeling more like professionals, and becoming more open with their intern over time and less anxious

Table 6.2

A Sample of Mentors' Ratings of the Mentoring Process

(i) Effectiveness of Mentor Workshops Reported as Percentages (N = 23)

Workshop	Extended Greatly	Extended Moderately	Extended Minimally	Did Not Extend
1. Observation as a Tool for Guidance	60.0	33.3	—	6.7
2. Classroom Management	46.2	46.2	—	7.6
3. Coaching Strategies	41.2	52.9	—	5.9
4. Postobservation Conference	53.3	46.7	—	—
5. Discipline and Motivation	28.6	64.3	—	7.1

(ii) Mentors' Perceptions of the Degree of Help Needed by Interns Reported as Percentages (N = 23)

Items	Very Much Help	Moderate Help	Little Help	No Help
1. Coordination of Classroom Activities	33.3	20.0	46.7	—
2. Assessment of Needs of Children	25.0	31.3	43.7	—
3. Suggestions for Curriculum	33.3	40.0	26.7	—
4. Suggestions for Management	46.7	33.3	20.0	—
5. Positive Coaching	50.0	32.0	14.3	—

(iii) Mentors' Ratings of Own Growth Reported as Percentages (N = 23)

Items on Mentor's Growth	Strongly Agree	Agree	Disagree	Strongly Disagree
1. I feel more like a professional	57.1	35.7	7.1	—
2. I became more open with my intern	53.3	46.7	—	—
3. I became less anxious about my work	31.3	62.5	—	6.2
4. I became more responsible in my job	25.0	43.8	25.0	6.2
5. I understand better the needs of others	25.0	68.0	6.2	—

about their own work. They became more positive about teaching and understood the needs of others better as they engaged in the mentoring process. In other items not shown in the table, mentors also reported a greater sense of responsibility and security in their jobs.

Interns' Ratings

Table 6.3 provides a sample of interns' perceptions of the mentoring process. In section (i), when interns were asked to indicate the degree of help they needed in key areas of teaching, they revealed that they considered themselves to be fairly competent in the areas of coordination of activities and assessment of needs. Their ratings in these two areas were supported by their mentors' ratings of them. However, on the next three items, interns perceived themselves as being more competent than was indicated by the ratings of others. Mentors and college professors reported giving more help in those last three areas than interns perceived themselves receiving.

In section (ii) of table 6.3, it is reported that interns regarded the mentoring process to be mostly positive. They enjoyed and appreciated the collegiality and support they received, and felt that they gained confidence over time. Section (iii) reveals that interns considered it very important to have someone listen to them, offer suggestions, and share ideas with them. Learning about classroom management and dealing with parents were also important to interns. Interns also gave high ratings to items related to the importance of having financial aid and being able to complete the master's degree program. Perhaps a key to retention of urban teachers is the provision of professional and financial support until they have obtained permanent certification.

Principals' Ratings

Principals in District 4, Manhattan, were asked to rate all mentored and unmentored teachers in their third year of teaching on several aspects of personal and professional behaviors. The instrument was an

Table 6.3
A Sample of Interns' Ratings of the Mentoring Process

(i) Interns' Perceptions of Degree of Help Needed in Key Areas of Teaching; Reported as Percentages (N = 45)

Items	Very Much Help	Moderate Help	Little Help	No Help
1. Coordination of Classroom Activities	28.9	17.8	48.9	4.4
2. Assessment of Needs of Children	26.1	38.1	33.3	2.4
3. Suggestions for Curriculum	26.7	40.0	33.3	—
4. Suggestions for Management	42.9	16.7	33.3	7.1
5. Positive Coaching	46.7	24.4	26.7	2.2

(ii) Interns' Perceptions of the Mentoring Process; Reported as Percentages (N = 45)

Items	Strongly Agree	Agree	Disagree	Strongly Disagree
1. Mentor provided sufficient feedback	37.2	53.5	6.9	2.3
2. I felt comfortable with personnel both in school and Hunter	42.2	55.6	—	2.2
3. I felt like a colleague of my mentor	54.5	36.4	6.8	—
4. Feedback was always provided	36.4	56.8	6.8	—
5. I appreciated the interactions with other interns	50.0	47.6	2.4	—

(iii) Interns' Ratings of the Importance of Various Aspects of the Mentoring Relationship; Reported as Percentages (N = 45)

Items	IMPORTANCE			
	Very	Great	Some	No
1. Having someone listen to me	65.9	34.1	—	—
2. Having mentor do demonstration lessons	39.5	32.6	25.6	2.3
3. Growing in confidence because of support	40.0	51.1	8.9	—
4. Seeing different teaching styles	63.6	29.5	6.8	—
5. Getting curriculum ideas	56.8	31.8	11.4	—

adapted version of a New York City Board of Education Rating Scale. The adapted rating scale included items from an earlier principals' questionnaire developed in this program. Table 6.4 provides samples of the results of these ratings.

For almost all items, principals rated mentored teachers' performance as outstanding or good. For unmentored teachers, high percentages were recorded mostly in the categories of "satisfactory" and "unsatisfactory." In section (i), Personal and Professional Qualities, the contrast is especially vivid on items that relate to the use of english, professional attitude and professional growth, and resourcefulness and initiative. No mentored teacher received an unsatisfactory rating on any of the seven items in this section, while unmentored teachers received four unsatisfactory ratings. The difference in principals' perceptions of mentored and unmentored teachers is most dramatic in section (ii) of the questionnaire, Pupil Guidance and Instruction. In each item of this section, principals' ratings of the performance of unmentored teachers as satisfactory or unsatisfactory exceeded 50 percent. The opposite was true for mentored teachers. Mentored teachers used positive methods to control their class much more frequently than unmentored teachers. For the item related to making curriculum interesting to children, the average rating of outstanding or good for mentored teachers was 86 percent, compared to 45 percent for unmentored teachers. When judging the extent of pupil participation (not included in this table), principals' percentage ratings were 87 percent for mentored teachers and 42.8 percent for unmentored teachers. For item c, evidence of children's growth in knowledge, skills, appreciations, and attitude, the relative percentages for mentored and unmentored teachers were 68 percent and 40 percent respectively.

In sections (iii) and (iv), similar patterns in the ratings of "outstanding" and "good" were observed for mentored and unmentored teachers. In section (iii), Classroom Management, the ratings on organization and attractiveness of room were 72 percent for mentored teachers but only 47.6 percent for unmentored teachers. In section (iv), which dealt with ability to maintain good relations with

Table 6.4

Principals' Ratings of Mentored and Unmentored Teachers
Reported as Percentages (N: M = 45, UNM = 23)

Items	MENTORED N = 45				UNMENTORED N = 23			
	Outstanding to Unsatisfactory							
	4	3	2	1	4	3	2	1
(i) Personal and Professional Qualities								
a. Use of English	41.3	43.6	15.1	—	5.3	47.7	36.8	10.5
b. Professional attitude and professional growth	42.2	40.0	17.6	—	13.1	34.8	39.1	13.0
c. Resourcefulness and initiative	56.0	22.0	22.0	—	19.1	23.8	47.6	9.5
(ii) Pupil Guidance and Instruction								
a. Use of positive methods to control class	51.6	29.7	16.3	—	19.1	28.5	33.3	19.1
b. Making curriculum interesting	28.4	57.1	14.2	—	10.1	35.0	35.0	20.0
c. Evidence of children's growth in knowledge, skills, attitudes	33.8	33.8	32.4	—	13.6	27.3	40.9	18.2
(iii) Classroom Management								
a. Organization and attractiveness	35.1	35.1	27.1	2.4	9.5	38.1	33.3	19.0
b. Routines for care of equipment	28.7	44.7	24.2	2.4	9.5	38.1	33.3	19.0
c. Attention to records and reports	18.7	45.1	33.8	2.4	14.3	38.1	33.3	14.3
(iv) Participation in School and Community Activities								
a. Maintaining good relations with colleagues	42.0	43.1	14.7	—	9.1	40.9	40.9	9.3
b. Establish and maintain relations with parents	30.4	52.4	17.1	—	13.6	36.4	36.4	13.6
c. Willingness to accept special assignments	44.4	42.9	10.4	—	13.6	36.4	45.5	4.5

colleagues, mentored teachers again received much higher ratings than unmentored ones. A similar pattern was seen in the other two items of this section. No mentored teacher received an unsatisfactory rating on any item in the final section of the principals' rating scale.

Conclusions

Apart from the quantitative information that illustrates various positive aspects of the program, several additional benefits were realized through this collaborative effort. A Teacher Center for the use of mentors, interns, and the college community has been established at Hunter College. It provides a space for seminars that address the needs of new and continuing TOC participants. The Teacher Center also provides a space for the display of outstanding projects and bulletin boards from mentor teachers' and interns' classrooms. Mentors and interns also learned negotiation techniques when they accompanied project staff on trips to the state legislature in Albany to discuss the needs of the project.

In addition, the mentor selection process has resulted in the identification of outstanding teachers who, because of the recognition and encouragement they received as mentors, developed the confidence to apply for other career opportunities. Many have enrolled in education programs that led to certification in administration and supervision. Project staff are in the process of examining the impact of mentoring service on the career path decisions of mentors.

Further, a new network has developed between the mentor teachers and college personnel. Traditionally, college faculty have met with district administrators when planning school-based projects. With the use of this new network, the college faculty has direct access to principals and teachers in several schools. College personnel can offer suggestions and innovative ideas with the expectation that teachers will be able to implement them and become catalysts for change within a school. This is a big step away from the "ivory tower" model that still exists in many places.

Finally, the Teacher Opportunity Corps program network offers college professors firsthand knowledge of teaching conditions in New York City. College personnel have the opportunity to assess and revise curriculum and methods courses to meet the needs of beginning teachers in the 1990s.

With a retention rate of 90 percent in the past three years and the majority of these teachers coming from minority backgrounds, this kind of program offers much hope. Thirty teachers per year have been mentored at a cost of approximately one hundred and forty thousand dollars per year. When one considers the costs to children, parents, and administrators of the "revolving door" passage of teachers in inner-city schools, the program is very cost-effective. It is hoped that collaborative relationships of this nature will continue to benefit the college, administrators, teachers, children, and families whose lives are so profoundly affected by the teaching and learning process.

References

Darling-Hammond, L. (1984, September 2). Why our best and brightest don't teach anymore. *Los Angeles Times* (Part V), in *Education Week, 3.*

Haberman, M. (1988). Proposals for recruiting minority teachers: Promising practices and attractive detours. *Journal of Teacher Education, 39*(4), 38–44.

Huffman, G.; and Leak, S. (1986). Beginning teachers' perceptions of mentors. *Journal of Teacher Education, 37*(1), 22–25.

Huling-Austin, L. (1990). Squishy business. In T. M. Bey and C. T. Holmes, eds., *Mentoring: Developing successful new teachers.* VA Association of Teacher Educators.

New York Times. (1988, October 5). E1, B13.

Odell, S. J. (1986). A model university-school system collaboration in teacher-induction. *Kappa Delta Pi Record, 22*(4), 120–121.

————. (1991). Characteristics of beginning teachers in an induction context. In Reinhartz, J. ed,. *Teacher induction.* Washington, DC: National Education Association.

Pflaum, S. M.; and Abramson, T. (1989). Teacher assignment, hiring and preparation: Minority teachers in New York City. Paper presented at AERA, San Francisco, CA.

Schwartz, J. (1989). New directions or teacher leaders: Politics and programs. Paper presented at AERA, San Francisco, CA.

Shulman, L. S. (1986). Those who understand knowledge growth in teaching. *Educational Researcher, 15*(2), 4–14.

Tikunoff, W. J.; and Ward, B. A. (1987, June). Reducing instructional risk for LEP students; Increasing instructional effectiveness for LEP students. Instructional Effectiveness Seminar #5, Hunter College, NY.

Veenman, S. (1984). Perceived problems of beginning teachers. *Review of Educational Research, 54,* 143–178.

Ward, B. A.; and Tikunoff, W. J. (1987, October). New teacher retention in inner-city schools projects: Implementation study, Year I, SWRL, CA.

Yarger-Kane, G.; and Buck, C. L., eds. (1989). *Collaborative roles in teacher education.* Position Paper by COTE.

7. Mentoring as a University/Public School Partnership

MERNA JACOBSEN

In this chapter, Jacobsen reports the long-standing effects of the University of Northern Colorado and public schools in its vicinity to work together to improve teaching and the induction process. The theoretical view of mentoring program participants and components and program effectiveness are discussed.

> My experience has been better than I ever dreamed it would. I remember sitting in the orientation meeting feeling scared and unsure of myself. I was really afraid that I would never make it much less succeed. I have come to adore my class, I feel I have developed a wonderful rapport with them. I have overcome my fears and insecurities about classroom management.... I have gained the support I felt I needed from a principal. My confidence in my ability has doubled. This has been the hardest, most rewarding year of my life.
>
> (Partner teacher, 1988)

The fears and concerns of a beginning teacher provided in the testimony above have haunted those responsible for teacher preparation in public schools, universities, state and national organizations, and teacher associations. Waves of teacher shortages, coupled with societal attention and controversy focused on the quality of teaching, have brought an onslaught of research to identify and address the needs of the beginning teacher. One offshoot of the investigation into needs of teachers concerns induction and mentoring programs housed in state licensing departments, public schools at the building level or in district staff development offices, and colleges of education or centers for teacher preparation.

The University of Northern Colorado's Teacher Induction Partnership (TIP) Program was originated in 1973 under UNC's College of Education Teacher Education Center. The program was designed to address alarming dropout rates of teachers nationally, provide a framework for beginning teachers to enter the profession successfully, and foster interaction between the University and Colorado school districts. More recently, the program has been used by districts to creatively meld with the use of site-based management models. Since its inception, the program has dealt with approximately 600 students who are now classroom teachers, team leaders, and school administrators.

UNC's Teacher Education Center forms partnerships with public schools who provide year-long teaching assignments for partner teachers. All districts are within 80 miles of the university and range in student population size from 1,000 to 27,000. The program currently deals with two main candidate populations. The first is the beginning teacher whose only experience has been student teaching and who is now embarking upon the first full-time instructional position. The second is the reentry individual. This is the nontraditional student who may have been in education some years ago and has stepped away from the profession (to raise a family or pursue other career paths) and is seeking reentry support into a system they perceive as having changed significantly. The vast majority of teacher candidates are of upper academic ability (the average GPA for 74 1989–90 partner teachers was 3.43 on a 4.0 scale) with ages ranging from early twenties to early fifties. Each year 75–85 partner teachers are placed with an equal number of mentors chosen for participation in several Colorado schools. During the induction year partner teachers are assisted in the technical, managerial, and emotional challenges of the first year and are provided ample opportunity and resources to build a repertoire. The program's emphasis is on creating a safe setting for personal and professional growth, experimentation and reflection. Follow-up studies reveal that approximately 85 percent of teacher participants continue to teach in the year following their induction experience.

Several principles guide the continuous development and daily implementation of the program.

1. The knowledge, values, and experiences of school practitioners and higher education personnel are equally desirable in providing a broad base to address teacher needs as well as a balance between craft knowledge and theory.

2. Further, the conceptual focus of the program has evolved from perspectives gleaned from collaboration between the university and public schools and amidst differing opinions about the desirable characteristics of emerging teachers.

3. The selection, training, and role definition of support personnel are the shared responsibilities of the university and school districts.

4. Support behaviors give emphasis to holistic teacher development, skill competency, psychological stability, formulation of an educational philosophy, and reflective abilities.

5. Each component of the infrastructure contributes to program effectiveness and quality of experience only through highly structured definitions of roles and responsibilities of participants and sponsoring agencies, support, training, monitoring, and orchestrated events to foster interdependence.

6. Program design accounts for needed flexibility and contextual variants.

7. Research and evaluation are an inherent feedback loop for program development.

View of Mentoring

The mentoring component of the TIP program is based on the notion that assistance is more effective than assessment. The model is a departure from more traditional doctor/patient approaches in which the neophyte is diagnosed and prescribed a cure by a seemingly all-knowing master. Rather, the relationship between mentor and partner teacher is collegial. The quality of interactions hinge on relationship issues (trust, rapport, readiness to assist and be assisted) and the mentor's ability to draw out and respond to the individual needs of the teacher. The interdependence between the pair is based on their shared recognition of the complexity of the teaching act and mutual permission granted for the partner teacher to experience stages of growth. This expectation for an individualized step-by-step movement for teacher independence demands that mentors not only be selected and trained carefully, but that they possess the breadth of knowledge and depth of experience that enables them to problem solve, work effectively with another adult, and contribute to the growing repertoire of the beginning teacher. Testimonies like the following demonstrate that mentors translate these premises into action. "We began with me in a directive role, moved to a collaborative relationship, and are now at the point where I am very non-directive" and "... enhanced creativity, gained confidence, built strong 'teaming' bonds working together and sharing ideas."

Program Participants and Components

Components of the TIP program were chosen and structured to meet three objectives. First, a multifaceted approach is taken to provide a safe environment in which participating teachers can be assisted in having their needs met. Group opportunities, one-on-one coaching, informal interaction, field practice, academic course work, and assistant and assessment functions are dimensions of the TIP structure. Second, the support personnel adjust to the needs of individuals as the year progresses. Third, the TIP structure allows for problem solving and decision making to be shared among participants.

Participants

The Partner Teacher

During the induction year, partner teachers are full-time instructional leaders in the classroom. They are accepted as any other faculty member with sensitivity given to reduced load and needed support.

In addition to the teaching assignment, partner teachers engage in a number of professional development activities which are listed below.

A professional development plan. Each partner teacher, in collaboration with their mentor, writes a professional development plan (PDP) which states goals the individual wishes to accomplish during the induction year and the objectives for doing so. The PDP is used throughout the year to reference progress. Members of the support team adjust to changes in the teacher's levels of concerns. The PDP is used in a midyear perception check for progress between the partner teacher and field consultant. Often, beginning concerns are very different than those midway through the year. The PDP is an effective tool for beginning teachers to see themselves in a process rather than as a finished product.

A professional portfolio. At the onset of the induction experience, partner teachers begin collecting artifacts and formulating short narratives about their importance which will culminate in a portfolio (Uphoff 1989). This activity is utilized to stimulate self-assessment in beginning teachers. The portfolio provides a historical representation of the growth of an individual and a foundation for goal setting and reflection (Shulman 1988). Through portfolio use, the teacher is always a learner, causing introspection and understanding of how teachers think. It is a mechanism to share materials, ideas, and activities with colleagues or in an interview setting. The culminating event is an end-of-the-year conference at which participants present their work in small cohort groups facilitated by experienced educators who probe for evidence of teacher self-understanding.

Video and audiotape analysis. Each partner teacher completes an audiotape self-analysis according to the Low Inference Self-Assessment Measure (LISAM) (Freiberg 1987). In this process, the teacher is responsible for analyzing his or her performance in the classroom with focus on questioning, wait time, motivating set and closure, positive teacher statements, teacher use of student ideas, and student talk to teacher talk ratio. The audiotape experience is less threatening than the videotaping, which usually occurs later in the year.

Academic seminars and cohort groups. Partner teachers attend seminars which are a combination of required readings, presentations, and group sharing. Each group stays intact throughout the year. The development of cohesiveness and trust necessary for collegial sharing is at the crux of the TIP structure. Opportunity for personal sharing is formally engineered to combat the isolation resultant from the time-bound teaching day as well as overcome historical attitudes preventing teachers from seeking assistance (Rosenholtz & Kyle 1984).

The Support Team

Each partner teacher has a support team of three individuals: a university field consultant, a mentor teacher, and the building principal. Each person in the triad has clearly defined roles.

The university field consultant maintains a regular schedule of classroom observations with pre- and post-conferencing aimed at providing specific feedback. With each visit, consultants conference with the mentors and principals. In addition, they act as caretakers and facilitators of the support team. They are responsible for ensuring sustained support through one-on-one training with mentors, airing of concerns, and open communication between all parties. Consultants are responsible for establishing an environment of readiness for a collegial approach to teacher development. They also instruct the monthly seminar for the cohort group they have been assigned.

University staff members are trained in clinical supervision, methods of causing reflection, observation and data collection techniques, stages of teacher development, growth models, and intervention methods. As integral part of staff development is the sharing of case studies. Strategies for direct and non-direct approaches are discussed as well as the appropriate balance between formal and informal interaction in their unique role.

As past classroom practitioners, consultants provide a different representation of how university personnel are viewed by public school participants. They are able to break traditional barriers between the two institutions, link research with practice, and have a unique impact as an individual outside the school district.

The mentor is a full-time teacher, selected and employed by the school district, who is responsible for providing assistance on a daily basis. The mentoring component is based on the notion that assistance is more effective than assessment. Mentors, therefore, do not engage in evaluative processes. Each mentor/partner teacher pair create a working plan for the year from a provided audiotape and workbook requiring an identification of the nature of support to be given as well as the frequency of interaction. While mentors are encouraged to make classroom observations, the nature of interaction between most pairs is informal. Mentors share materials, act as sounding boards for ideas and concerns, accelerate the socialization process to the school and community, and facilitate relationships between the partner teacher and staff, parents, and students. The legal contract between UNC and partner districts stipulates that the mentor teacher must have (a) the willingness to work with a partner teacher, (b) sufficient time available to cooperate with district and program personnel in planning and implementing an acceptable induction experience for the partner teacher, and (c) at least three years of satisfactory experience in the profession.

Many districts offer in-house training for mentors. One district requires mentors to have documented evidence of formal training in supervisory skills. This same district pays their mentors a one thousand dollar annual stipend.

Mentors are chosen by principals. Selection criteria is based on current research on mentor/protege matches. For example, most mentors share a common planning period or are teaching within the same physical proximity and at the same age and subject level as their beginning teacher (Huling-Austin 1989).

The building principal is responsible for insuring a quality placement site. This individual sponsors the partner teacher in the district assessment model, conducting cycles of observations tied to formative and summative evaluations.

Principal roles vary. For example, some principals meet with partner teachers weekly for informal sharing. Others see themselves as ambassadors for induction, working to insure acceptance of the beginning teacher and the concepts of the program.

Components

Orientations

All groups of the support team—partner teachers, mentors, and principals—are provided orientations. Program expectations, descriptions of roles and responsibilities, and information about the national movement toward induction are provided.

A day-long orientation for partner teachers is held prior to the onset of the teaching assignment. Workshops on such topics as getting organized for instruction, classroom management, current trends in education, decision making in a multicultural classroom, and communication skills for teachers are presented. Partner teachers also meet with their field consultant and engage in activities that serve as the foundation for the interaction that will occur in their cohort groups the coming year. Partner teachers are given an overview of the year and meet with former program participants in an informal setting to ask questions and glean a perspective on others' experiences.

The orientation for mentors includes a description of the behaviors and support they can give the beginning teacher. Rationale is provided for the emphasis on assistance rather than assessment functions of the mentor. The relationship between mentor, principal, and field consultant is explored. Mentors are provided biographical materials on the field consultant, a topic list of resources that can be provided for them pertaining to mentoring, and suggested do's and don'ts for mentors.

Principals are oriented as to their role in monitoring the conditions of the placement sites, sponsoring the beginning teachers in the districts' assessment model, and what they can expect from the university partnership.

Graduate Seminars

Seminars are delivered in the partner districts for partner teachers and mentors.

Topics are predetermined and sequenced based on the current trends in teacher education. Seminar topics include management systems, special needs students, teacher stress and burnout, learning styles and teaching strategies, and communication. A packet of materials taken from current research is provided for each seminar. The interdependence and cohesiveness among group members creates a safe environment for airing concerns and generating strategies applicable to specific situations. Emphasis is placed on reflection and mirroring as part of confirming ideas, concerns, and philosophies, and interaction that solidifies the values and convictions of the teacher.

The university program offers an optional course for mentors that provides training in techniques of analysis of instruction, approaches to conferencing, feedback skills, establishing trust, and relationship and rapport building. There is an interchange between skills learned in class and application to the field setting. Mentors explore the usability of skills and information in interaction with the partner teacher and process in class in the form of critical incident writing and case study discussion. Mentors act as a support group for each other.

The University/Public School Partnership

Each district has a representative contact person who is responsible for negotiating legal contracts and defining the appropriate use of the program in a given district. The university hosts an annual forum for contact persons to share evaluative data and solicit input for program development. The forum fosters interdependence and networking among public school representatives. These representatives exchange models of unique uses of the program and glean ideas for future directions. The contact person's forum is a key "linking pin" in fostering induction in a state where it is not mandated.

The program is funded solely by monies from public schools. That money pays each partner teacher a stipend (which is roughly half the salary of a regular contract beginning teacher), the tuition for 10 semester hours of graduate credit, and all salaries and operational costs of the program. The program relies on the public school partnership as it does not receive monies from the university, nor does it receive state funding.

The partnership also includes a university relationship with district staff development projects. School district personnel are often asked to assist in teaching the monthly seminars. In one district, staff development personnel plan and deliver one of the seminars. There are also special events, planned and implemented jointly by the university and partner districts. For example, consultant Leslie Huling-Austin presented a program on induction for all schools. This was sponsored by the program and one participating district.

Placement sites are the foundation of the university/public school partnership. Three-fourths of partner teachers are placed through standard procedures, that is, positions are identified by building principals and teachers are chosen from the hiring pool. The remainder are part of one of three unique facets of the TIP program.

A professional renewal program. Openings are created when master teachers are released to supervise student teachers and instruct methods courses at the university. The district continues to pay the master teachers' salary and the university provides a partner teacher free of charge to fill the resultant opening. The program is designed to provide additional professional opportunities for the experienced educator, create a quality placement site for a beginning teacher, and strengthen relationships between the university and public schools.

The preservice elementary science/mathematics project. Each year the project identifies master teachers from Colorado schools who are released from the classroom to develop math and science curriculum at the university. These individuals team-teach methods and content courses with professors and create materials and inservice trainings they can take back to their home districts. Not only do districts receive added support for math and science, but classroom teachers are transformed into district leaders. University students and professors are benefited by practitioner role models. The project is funded in part by the National Science Foundations. The Foundation pays the TIP program the cost of the partner teacher.

Teacher on special assignment (TOSA) projects. Openings are created when master teachers accept unique leadership roles in buildings or at the district administration level. For example, many principals release master teachers to incorporate new projects or systems into the staff, conduct in-services, develop materials, and coordinate events. These individuals then mentor the partner teacher placed in the resultant classroom opening. In one district the TOSA and partner teacher share the classroom for a half day, and the partner teacher assumes the balance of the day while the master teacher attends to special assignments. The district is responsible for all costs. An increase in the number of placements of this nature has occurred with the cultivation of site-based management models.

Selection and Screening Procedures

Each year approximately 600 teachers make requests for application. Of these, 200–250 will complete the process.

Participants are accepted on the basis of GPA (minimum 2.75), a writing sample, acceptance into the UNC Graduate School, and oral interviews. Applicants must be fully certified. With the completion of an application packet (credentials, an essay describing their desire and suitability for the program, applications), the candidate begins the interview process. The first oral interview is with university personnel. Candidates are provided program information and suitability for acceptance is determined. If approved by this interview, the candidate identifies the districts to which the packet should be sent for further consideration. District personnel administrators then screen applicants according to district criteria. For example, one district requires a 3.0 minimum GPA, another requires each candidate to complete a teacher perceiver interview. The final leg of the interview process comes at the building level. Here the candidate may interview with a principal or a team of teachers including the mentor. One or more interviews may occur at this stage. The final selection of a candidate in the placement process is made by the building principal and teachers.

This shared authority in the selection and screening of candidates insures ownership and support of the program and its participants at all levels of those involved.

Considerations for Program Conceptualization and Implementation

The examination of induction has led to discussions about the constructs of such programs. Powell (1988) identified candidate selection, supportive environment, and professional environment as key elements in program design. Odell (1987) associated program characteristics to sponsoring agents. For example, programs originating from state licensing boards concentrate on evaluative actions designed to screen out the least desirable teachers. Programs originating from school districts tend to be short in duration and emphasize orienting the new teacher. Programs hosted by universities are concerned more with educating the beginning teacher through course work.

Other writings on induction have attempted to review the broad spectrum of design and implementation of programs nationally (Rauth & Bowers 1986). This attempt to corral the variety of practices and philosophies has produced a laundry list of purposes of an induction program. Providing support heads the list with a number of variations (system information, resources and materials, instructional techniques, emotional support, classroom management, environment, demonstration teaching) (Odell 1986). Hegler and Dudley (1987) summarized the work of Huling-Austin (1986), Johnston (1985), Odell (1986), and Fox and Singletary (1986) for a broader list of purposes including: improvement of teacher performance, increased teacher retention rates, greater personal and professional well-being for the beginning teacher, increased knowledge and skills, satisfaction of induction related requirements for certification, illumination of issues, development of attitudes related to effective teaching, and orientation of the new teacher and sharing of cultures. Varah, Theune, and Parker (1986) took the purpose of induction to an even higher level when they charged that a program should raise the competency levels of participants distinctly above that of the beginning teacher and develop an individual teaching style based on observation, discussion, and consultation. Odell (1987) capsulized the purpose of the structured induction program when she stated that it is to offer interventions that will deal with the "collapse of the ideals they formed about teaching during teacher training" (p. 70).

In response to the dialogue centering on induction, 11 states have mandated some kind of induction program for school districts and 21 other states are either planning or piloting induction efforts (Hawk & Robards 1987). The Holmes Group (1986), the Carnegie Forum (1986), and NCATE (cited in Association of Teacher Educators 1986) all promote some form of residencies or internships.

Regardless of contextual considerations, sponsoring agent, or intended focus, program implementers may be faced with certain integral issues.

Induction Design and Implementation in the Absence of State Mandated Policy

Effective mentoring/induction programs can exist in states where legislative bodies and state departments have not mandated policies and expectations by considering the following conditions and procedures.

Systematic Educational Campaigns

In order for induction programs to operate successfully, there must be awareness and acceptance from participants. UNC's TIP program conducts ongoing educational functions for public school, university, and state personnel that include:

1. A monthly communication piece with a circulation that includes possible state policymakers, potential school district participants, former participants, and current mentors, principals, and partner teachers. The purpose of the newsletter is to provide regular, predictable interaction, provide information about induction substantiated by research, relate models in operation nationally, clarify policies and procedures, and spotlight program participants.

2. Orientations for partner teachers, mentors, and principals, including an overview on the importance and effectiveness of induction.

3. Face-to-face meetings with public school administration that are held in both participant and nonparticipant districts during the recruiting season.

4. Materials containing current research, suggestions for an enriched induction experience, and clarification of program policies and procedures. A program handbook, audiotapes, orientation videos, and workbooks are all part of the educational campaign.

5. Special events to provide information or recognition that may be hosted by the university or partner districts.

Collaborative Models

Programs that seek partnerships between agencies can pool resources and ideas. The TIP program is able to draw from public schools and the university for curricular material, staffing, facilities, contrasting educational cultures and values, and a broad base for sponsoring induction growth and development in the state. A collaborative approach causes individuals and organizations to decenter, examining the other parties' culture and values toward induction. This investment of time can diminish traditional barriers and competition, result in better decision making, build a knowledge base, and reap greater benefits for the beginning teacher. For example, in the event that a teacher is struggling, input from school practitioners and university personnel can provide a balanced perspective for intervention, remediation, or exit counseling. Conversely, successful teachers have a host of advocates working on their behalf in the hiring process.

Creative Funding and Reward Systems

Current trends toward site-based management and teacher empowerment can allow for greater flexibility for funding induction and mentoring programs. Several schools provide funding for the program through teacher/principal written grants. In the absence of state mandates, it may be difficult to provide remuneration for mentor teachers. Through the district/university partnership approach, mentors may be eligible for tuition benefits from the university or some form of faculty status.

Linkage to Pre-service and In-service

The greatest challenge for an induction/mentoring program grounded in a university/school district context of collaboration remains one of merging different perceptions about the nature and value of such efforts and creating a shared knowledge base functional in all participants. Induction, then, becomes a "linking pin" between pre- and in-service functions. This forced dialogue erodes a traditional approach to teacher education in which public schools and institutions of higher education acted as separatists, and provides legitimacy to the experiences and knowledge gained in both worlds.

Balancing Flexibility with Consistency and Uniformity

A partnership presumes different behaviors than if universities and public schools initiate mentoring programs as soloists: (a) there will be shared authority issues, (b) expectations for design and delivery must be negotiated, (c) program development is a collaborative effort, and (d) differences in educational values and approaches will continually shape the relationship among participants.

The complex nature of partnerships in educational endeavors, coupled with a knowledge base about induction in its infancy, can lead to an array of interpretations and applications of roles and responsibilities. While flexibility is crucial in a university-sponsored field-based program, a basic structure designed to protect key elements is essential.

Selection and Training of Mentors

Mentor selection based on the criteria mentioned earlier prevents their identification and involvement based solely on personal friendship, political considerations, or desires to provide a stimulating experience for a stagnate veteran teacher.

Consistency in mentor training insures that a collegial rather than supervisor/student approach is taken in the development of fully certified individuals. Mentoring connotes that a master teacher draws from professional experiences and shares with another adult in a peer relationship. It represents an advancement in the nature of support given beginning teachers, that is, professionals at different levels together confront problems of education that are not the sole province of the neophyte. For example, the demands placed on the beginning teacher because of the longevity of the assignment distinguishes it from preservice field experience settings. The peer relationship requires a broader window for discussion on areas of disagreement and greater tolerance for the evolution of an individual teaching style and philosophy for the beginning teacher influenced by, but independent of, the mentor's approach. Through mentor training, a university program has the opportunity and responsibility for on-going staff development within each building, fostering master teachers who can cause growth in a beginning teacher as well as reflect on their own performance.

Identification of Quality Placement Sites

The placement site is the source of the most comfort or threat for the beginning teacher. It is here that the novice will begin to formulate habits that may last a lifetime. Their philosophy and self-esteem as an educator will be impacted by the quality of relationships they form, the level of professional performance they witness, and the successful educational and personal events they design and implement.

Current research is firm about the characteristics of sites most conducive to a successful first year. Strong support personnel with attention given to common planning period, close proximity to the beginning teacher, and same teaching assignments as criteria for making mentor/protege matches are important. Additionally, protecting the beginner from difficult teaching settings—high student/teacher ratios, several preparations, too many out-of-class responsibilities, assignment to teach subjects outside one's area of certification—is paramount in the identification of suitable sites (Huling-Austin 1989).

But a quality placement site is more than logistics and support. It is also tied to the attitudes and culture of a particular building. Awareness and acceptance about induction among staff and parents is essential. Public school practitioners must see themselves as sharing in the professional responsibility of preparing new teachers. Collegial interaction should be evident—built into the scheme of getting things done. This fosters a nurturing atmosphere in which the novice is free to seek help without judgment or fear of failure. The principal's role in protecting the integrity of placement sites is exemplified by one who felt her building should not be used in the immediate future. "Not at this time. There has been an environment of conflict among staff members. This needs to be resolved before teachers here can be supportive for someone new."

Mentoring as Impetus for Beginning Teachers to Act as Change Agents vs. Perpetuators of the Status Quo

While the socialization of new teachers is an honorable goal for any induction/mentoring program, implementers may be faced with questions concerning a program's ability to develop teachers capable of acting comfortably in change agent roles. Such questions might include: What conditions must be inherent at the placement site? How would selection and screening of candidates be different? Are beginning teachers an appropriate population to consider for such a role? How would the support given beginning teachers differ? Program mission and goals should reflect the implementers' attitudes and values concerning the beginning teacher as facilitator of change.

Program Impact and Effectiveness

Each year mentors, principals, and partner teachers evaluate the program. Each group rates a number of items within major groupings that include support given the beginning teacher by mentor, field consultant, and principal, satisfaction with the program, quality of the placement site, and program strengths and weaknesses. Information particular to a group is also gathered in the evaluative process. Partner teachers provide preferences for several items related to program development. Mentors relate information concerning the structure of contact with the beginning teacher and preferred rewards. Principals reveal their reasons for participating in the program.

Important findings from evaluative data from the 1990 participants are provided below. Percentages given indicate those who rated
items as 4 or 5 on a scale of 1 to 5. On the evaluative instrument,
ratings of 1 and 2 represented that expectations were not met, and
ratings of 4 and 5 indicated that expectations were exceeded. A rating
of 3 represented a neutral response. One hundred percent of evaluations were returned from partner teachers, 73 percent from mentors,
and 63 percent from principals.

Support

Partner teachers rated the support given them by the university field
consultant higher than the support they received from the mentor or
principal. For example, 71 percent of partner teachers said the field
consultant made regular visits and observations, while only 33 percent felt the mentor did so, and 43 percent felt the principal ade-
quately observed them. When contrasting partner teacher ratings of
professional feedback on instruction given by field consultants, mentors, and principals, field consultants again received a greater percentage of higher ratings (75 percent) than mentors (55 percent) or
principals (50 percent). Other areas receiving high ratings for field
consultants concerned university staff being available and approachable (80 percent) and providing encouragement and emotional support (77 percent). These ratings may stem from several factors. First,
partner teachers may confide in a university consultant who, by position, is an unbiased observer, not caught in the day-to-day politics
and personalities of the immediate school setting. In other words, the
university consultant is a "safe" ear. Second, the nature of the consultant's position in the UNC model falls between assistance and assessment. That is, the consultant observes lessons, provides feedback,
conducts summative and formative evaluations, but is not necessarily
connected with the hiring process for any district. In this fashion,
even the assessment behaviors of a consultant are primarily for
teacher reflection. The consultant then has greater freedom to provide emotional support without compromising either assistance

or assessment functions. The higher ratings awarded university personnel may be resultant from inherent structural barriers in the design and delivery of the program—limited time for mentors to dedicate to the partner teacher who may have exaggerated expectations of an in-house support person, lack of consistency in clarification of the mentor's role, potential mentor/partner teacher mismatches, inconsistency in mentor training, or mentor's own idiosyncratic view of the role. These findings may have implications for programs using school district personnel rather than university staff in the consultant role.

Subsequent interviews with university field consultants provided clues as to their effectiveness.

> As a field consultant you yourself have to be creative and use what I call your intuition and diagnosing skills.... And another example of that is troubleshooting, anticipating things that need to be done, reading Partner Teachers effectively, and really getting to know their strengths and weaknesses as a person. Often you can translate that, you can see it in their classrooms. If you can really assess who they are and accept their strengths and weaknesses, you can take those strengths and build a dynamic teacher from them.

This recognition of needing to respond to partner teachers as individuals was echoed by another consultant. "Depending on the person you're working with it may be almost a prodding, pushing, like you've got a stone and you're rolling them along bit by bit. Others, it's like you're almost running to catch up with them."

Partner teachers rated several items concerning mentor support (Table 7.1). Mentors rated themselves on the same items. Both groups were in agreement about the areas of greatest support given by mentors; that is, sharing of materials, maintaining regular contact, establishing trust, and providing emotional support were rated high by both groups. Ratings differed in the areas of problem solving and providing assistance in understanding district curriculum. Partner teacher ratings of mentors in these categories were lower than mentor

Table 7.1

*Percentage of Ratings of Four or Five Given by Partner Teachers and
Mentors Regarding Mentor Support*

| | Percentages | |
| | Partner Teachers' | Mentors' |
Item	Rating of Mentors	Self-Rating
Provide orientation to school	57.3	68.5
Assist in understanding curriculum	50.7	75.9
Share materials and resources	72.0	85.5
Sponsor partner teachers in organizations	36.1	13.2
Maintain regular contact	74.7	88.9
Assist with professional development plan	23.3	37.7
Establish trust/respect	75.3	90.9
Assist with designing curriculum	39.2	55.5
Observe partner teachers in classroom	33.3	48.2
Provide developmental feedback	54.7	54.7
Discuss partner teachers with		
principal, consultant	56.1	60.0
Provide emotional support	74.7	85.4
Problem solve with partner teachers	68.0	79.6

self-ratings. Both groups agreed that mentors did not sponsor the partner teacher in professional organizations, nor were partner teachers
satisfied with the assistance received from mentors in developing a
professional development plan.

As seen in table 7.2, principals' self-ratings were higher than
partner teacher ratings of support given by principals. The only exception was in the area of troubleshooting where 82 percent of partner teachers felt their expectations of the principal were exceeded,
and 70 percent of principals felt they exceeded expectations in this
area. The items showing the greatest discrepancies concerned observations, discussion of qualifications for jobs, and the principal's role in
facilitating the mentor/partner teacher relationship. In all three instances, principals rated themselves higher than the partner teachers
rated them.

Perhaps the differences in these ratings are attributable to perceptions of what constitutes a meaningful interaction between principal

Table 7.2

Percentage of Ratings of Four or Five Given by Partner Teachers and Principals Regarding Principal Support

	Percentages	
Item	*Partner Teachers' Rating of Principal*	*Principals' Self-Rating*
Make regular visits/observations	42.6	74.5
Offer timely/meaningful feedback	50.0	57.4
Assist with troubleshooting	82.4	69.5
Inform partner teachers of district in-service/resources	45.3	69.5
Discuss partner teacher's qualifications and job opportunities	40.0	67.4
Facilitate partner teacher/mentor relationship	29.4	57.4

and partner teacher. A principal may feel much is gleaned by informal walk-throughs while the teacher may feel only a formal appointment constitutes an observation. The perceived lack of support related to job opportunities may be a function of the greatest concern for any first-year person—continued employment.

When principals were asked to rate the effectiveness of the university field consultants, 91 percent said their expectations were exceeded in the area of observation of the partner teachers' instructional performance. Ninety-one percent felt university personnel communicated in an approachable manner and shared perceptions about the partner teacher. Similarly, 89 percent said field consultants exceeded expectations in assisting with resolving concerns. Comments gleaned from principals indicated that they were influenced by the frequency and regularity of site visits from university personnel. This perception of availability may account for the high ratings.

Satisfaction with the Program

Eighty-seven percent of partner teachers said involvement in the program enhanced their skills, and 71 percent said it caused them to reflect on their performance. Eighty percent of partner teachers said they would participate in the program again. Support from university and school district staff was reported as the greatest strength of the program by partner teachers. This same group sited increased self-confidence as the aspect of their professional growth enhanced the most by participation, as well as insights into the inner workings of school systems.

Nearly three-fourths of mentors reported being satisfied with the program, and 88 percent said they would mentor again. In fact, data revealed that mentors felt their skills as teachers were enhanced. "We worked extremely well together which enabled us both to learn a lot" and "It was a two-way street. She promoted new ideas in me as well as I promoted, in a supportive way, knowledge, confidence, and experience" are testimonies indicative of the positive impact participation in the program has on the mentor. This group also felt their efforts influenced the beginning teacher. One mentor described her contributions as "Honest feedback, plans for professional growth, a safer place to develop versus baptism by fire." Mentors and principals share partner teachers perceptions that the support given the beginning teacher is the greatest strength of the program.

Principal ratings concerning satisfaction with the program were among the highest reported. Ninety-six percent said their expectations were exceeded, and 100 percent said they would recommend it to other administrators.

Satisfaction with Placement Site

One of the most startling findings from the evaluative data concerned ratings of placement sites (Table 7.3). Partner teachers, mentors, and principals disagreed sharply about willingness of mentors to work with beginning teachers, conditions that make for a beneficial experience, and overall satisfaction with the school as a placement site. Principals rated the latter two items higher with mentors giving the willingness of mentors to work with beginning teachers their highest scores. The three groups generally agreed that placement sites offered

Table 7.3
*Percentage of Ratings of Four or Five Given by Partner Teachers, Mentors,
and Principals Regarding Quality of Placement Site*

| Item | Percentages | | |
	Partner Teachers	Mentors	Principals
Support for partner teachers	72.0	73.0	85.1
Understanding of TIP program	45.3	47.2	57.4
Willingness of mentors to work with partner teachers	68.0	82.7	74.5
Conditions for a beneficial experience	64.0	76.9	85.1
Recommend as future site	67.6	79.5	85.1

support for the beginning teacher, but that there was little under-standing of the induction program at the site.

Table 7.3 may represent an egocentric interpretation of one's contributions and domains of responsibilities. In order to protect their investment of time and energy, regardless of how meaningful it is viewed by the partner teacher, it seems that mentors and principals must rate themselves high. Or perhaps understanding of the partner teachers' dilemma by mentors and principals does not match the be-ginners' expectations of the quality of support that will be given.

Program Development

Program structure and delivery are continuously reviewed through formal and informal processes to respond to current trends in induc-tion, recent research, and university expectations for academic integ-rity. Partner teachers were asked to give ratings reflecting their preference for several possible program changes. In general, re-sponses indicated opposition to increased academic responsibilities and more frequent contacts with the field consultant and seminar group. Only 28 percent were in favor of the year culminating in a master's degree. Similarly, only 32 percent wanted to increase academic classes during the year thereby increasing graduate credits earned. Sixty-eight percent favored visits by the university field consultant every three to four weeks while only 15 percent wanted the consultant to observe them at least once per week. Only one-fourth of respondents indicated a desire for seminars twice per month rather than the extant monthly meetings. The message from beginning teachers is clear. The time for classroom preparation and performance is ferociously protected. Regardless of the possible future benefits from increased academic endeavors, most prefer to concentrate on the here and now.

Mentor Findings

Slightly more than half of mentors reported they had a common planning period which was used for conferencing with the partner teacher. More frequently mentioned were before and after school (71 percent) and lunch time (67 percent) as time spent between mentor and beginning teacher.

   Mentors were asked to rate incentives for them to mentor again. Eighty-nine percent preferred monetary rewards. Partner teachers similarly supported remuneration for mentors. State-sponsored credit for recertification was also highly rated by mentors (82 percent). Free tuition for university courses and release time were favored by slightly more than half of the respondents. Only 40 percent of mentors indicated that district recognition would be motivating to them.

Principal Motivation

Creative staffing was reported by principals as their primary reason for participating in the program (83 percent). Slightly more than half were motivated by the opportunity to reduce class size for several teachers in a building. Approximately half of the principals indicated a concern for providing a site for beginning teacher training.

Chapter Summary

The University of Northern Colorado's Teacher Induction Program forms partnerships with Colorado school districts who provide placement sites for beginning teachers. The program is not related to licensure and currently no centralized state format or expectation exists. The program model includes (a) orientations for mentors, principals, and partner teachers; (b) graduate seminars for partner teachers; (c) a three-person support team consisting of a university field consultant, on-site mentor teacher, and principal; (d) legal contracts between all parties stipulating roles and responsibilities; (e) graduate courses for mentors; (f) full-time university staff who conduct regular classroom observations and instruct seminars; (g) activities designed to develop reflective abilities in the beginning teacher such as professional portfolios and professional development plans; (h) specifically designed collaborative efforts between the university and public schools. The mentoring component of the TIP program is based on assistance rather than assessment, interdependence between the pair, and a collegial approach to communication. Cohort groups play an essential role, fostering the trust and cohesiveness necessary for beginning teachers to feel comfortable in seeking assistance. Follow-up studies indicate retention rates of participating teachers in the year following the induction experience are approximately 85 percent. Evaluative data reveal greater percentages of higher ratings reported for the support given the partner teacher by the university field consultant than by the mentor or principal. Further, partner teachers reported that participation in the program enhanced their skills and caused them to reflect on their performance. Mentors also indicated a reciprocal positive impact on their teaching resultant from assisting a beginning teacher. Highest satisfaction ratings with the program were reported from principals.

References

Association of Teacher Education Blue Ribbon Task Force. (1986). *Visions of reform: Implications for the education profession.* Reston, VA: Association of Teacher Educators.

Carnegie Task Force on Teaching as a Profession. (1986). *A nation prepared: Teachers for the twenty-first century.* New York: Carnegie Forum on Education and the Economy, Carnegie Corporation.

Fox, S. M.; and Singletary, T. J. (1986). Deductions about supportive induction. *Journal of Teacher Education, 37*(1), 12–15.

Frieberg, H. J. (1987). Teacher self-evaluation and principal supervision. *NASSP Bulletin, 71*(498), 85–92.

Hawk, P.; and Robards, S. (1987). Statewide teacher induction programs. In D. M. Brooks, ed., *Teacher induction: A new beginning.* Reston, VA: Association of Teacher Educators.

Hegler, K.; and Dudley, R. (1987). Beginning teacher induction: A progress report. *Journal of Teacher Education, 38*(1), 53–56.

Holmes Group Executive Board. (1986). *Tomorrow's teachers: A report of the Holmes Group.* East Lansing, MI: Holmes Group.

Huling-Austin, L. (1986). What can and cannot reasonably be expected from teacher induction programs. *Journal of Teacher Education, 37*(1), 2–5.

———. (1989, January). Making it past Christmas: Assisting the first year teacher. Paper presented at a Forum on Teacher Induction sponsored by the Colorado Council of Deans of Education, Denver, CO.

Johnston, J. (1985). Teacher induction: Problems, roles, and guidelines. In P. Burke and R. Heideman, eds., *Career-long teacher education.* Springfield, IL: Charles C. Thomas.

Odell, S. J. (1986). Induction support of new teachers: A functional approach. *Journal of Teacher Education, 37*(1), 26–29.

———. (1987). Teacher induction: Rationale and issues. In D. M. Brooks, ed., *Teacher induction: A new beginning.* Reston, VA: Association of Teacher Education.

Powell, A. G. (1988). Internships in independent schools: What can be learned from them? *Colloquy 1*(2), 5–10.

Rauth, M.; and Bowers, G. R. (1986). Reactions to induction articles. *Journal of Teacher Education, 37*(1), 38–41.

Rosenholtz, S. J.; and Kyle, S. J. (1984). Teacher isolation: Barrier to professionalism. *American Educator, 8*(4), 10–15.

Shulman, L. S. (1988). A union of insufficiencies: Strategies for teacher assessment in a period of educational reform. *Educational Leadership, 46*(3), 36–41.

Uphoff, J. K. (1989). Portfolio development and use: The why's, how's, and what's. Paper presented at the American Association of Colleges for Teacher Education, Chicago, IL.

Varah, L. J.; Theune, W. S.; and Parker, L. (1986). Beginning teachers: Sink or swim? *Journal of Teacher Education, 37*(1), 30–33.

Part III

Lessons and Questions Evolving from Research and Practice

This part provides the reader with two important things. First, it presents the results of a large-scale study that gathers the opinions of experienced mentors regarding items they judged to be helpful in the process of mentoring. Second, the final chapter organizes some of the major lessons and questions that are raised by the practice reports in the components of this book. This concluding chapter is not intended as an ending, but rather as a beginning—a starting place for the more specific questions and lessons you the reader will undoubtedly raise when you reflect upon this volume.

8. Mentor Suggestions for Establishing Mentor Teacher Programs

GARY P. DEBOLT

The results of a large-scale Delphi Study of elements reported to be helpful in mentoring, the characteristics of mentors, activities of mentoring, and elements of organizational structure, served as the foci for the study. This chapter is a research report that draws upon the opinions of experienced mentor teachers from twenty-eight mentoring projects from all parts of New York State. The results of this study can serve to confirm "good" practice or to direct efforts in the establishment of new programs.

Preface

Do you remember when you wanted to learn to drive a car? There were lots of people who knew how to do it. They could show you. You could read about it, watch others do it, or watch it being done on TV. There were even specific courses in school to teach you the theories involved in the process and to allow you to practice your new skills under the watchful guidance of a trained instructor.

As adults, most of us have mastered the skills of driving. Some were "naturals" and learned almost instantly. Others took more time, more support, more practice. Over the years, driving has become almost second nature to many of us. We seldom think about it; we just do it.

Recently, while visiting my best friend from high school, I experienced a very powerful realization. My friend's younger son, Casey, was finishing a basketball game at the community recreation center. Michael, who had recently received his driver's permit, was about to leave to pick up his younger brother. My friend's wife, Kathy, said,

---

*Portions of this chapter were previously presented in: Debolt, G. (1989). *Helpful elements in the mentoring of first-year teachers.* Unpublished dissertation. Syracuse, NY: Syracuse University.

"Gary, why don't you go with him?" So I did. As we drove, it occurred to me that this was a new role for me.

Once, I had been a new driver. My mother and sister had been my teachers. For years after that, I had been an independent driver. I had driven for many years, seldom really thinking about what it was I was doing. Now, for the first time, I found myself in the new role of being a guide, or helper, to a beginning driver. I found myself wondering if I would be able to explain, assist, or support this young friend as he developed his new skills and confidence.

Later, I discussed my feeling with Michael's father, Dan. He shared many of his experiences as a "driving instructor" with me. As we talked, I learned that I was not unique to have had doubts and uncertainties when I was in this new role. Dan reassured me and provided some insight into how he had dealt with the task of helping his son learn to drive. It was very worthwhile to share with someone who had already experienced what was so new to me. I was well aware that in a few short years, my own son will be getting his permit!

In many ways helping someone to learn to drive is like mentoring a new teacher. Each involves a helping, supportive role. Sometimes, a close personal relationship is strengthened by the joint efforts to help the novice develop competence and self-confidence in this new role. Certainly each new role is complex—each being composed of both science and art; and the goal of each association is to develop independence in the novice.

Introduction

As discussed earlier in this volume, educators have been concerned with the difficulties represented by the first year of teaching. The first year of teaching has been cited as: a source of discouragement (Ryan et al. 1980); a confrontation with reality (Veenman 1984); and a time of transition (Mager 1986). Support of new teachers is crucial during their initial experience (Galvez-Hjornevik 1986). One way of providing such support is to match experienced teachers serving as mentors with first-year teachers.

In the spring of 1986, New York State enacted legislation establishing a program aimed at assisting local school districts in developing support for beginning teachers as they made the transition from preparation to practice. The support was to be provided by successful, experienced teachers serving as mentors for the first-year interns. In 1986–1987, twenty-four local mentor teacher-internship projects were funded by the State. Seventy-nine local projects were funded as part of the Mentor Teacher-Internship (MTI) Program for the 1990–1991 school year. The state budgeted $16.5 million to support these projects.

From the inception of the MTI Program in 1986, the State Education Department of New York worked with Gerald M. Mager of Syracuse University to conduct a statewide evaluation of the various local projects as they were conceptualized and implemented across the state. The study reported here was an outgrowth of questions raised during the early stages of that statewide evaluation.

Purpose

A content review of the original twenty-four project proposals funded in 1986 led to questions regarding vagueness with which local project planners described mentoring. The proposed processes for identifying, training, or supporting prospective mentor teachers were lacking in clarity and consensus.

The purpose of this study was to elicit and to organize the experiences of a large group of teachers who had served as mentors. Each individual mentor, within his or her own specific context, was asked to consider the workings of the mentoring process. The study sought to use the reflections of the mentors to reach a consensus, or general opinion, regarding the following research question: What are the elements identified by experienced mentors that are helpful in the mentoring of first-year teachers?

Review of the Literature

The literature on mentoring of first-year teachers continues to grow. Concern has been expressed for the vague definitions of the terms *mentor* and *mentoring* (Anderson & Shannon 1988, Thies-Sprinthall 1986, Gray & Gray 1985). Studies have examined both informal mentoring among teachers (Gehrke & Kay 1984, Egan 1985) and formalized mentoring of novice teachers (Hoffman et al. 1986, Showers 1984).

A review of the literature on mentoring further confirmed that there were no widely accepted guidelines to help planners of mentoring programs develop strategies to provide training, understanding of the process of mentoring, and support for teachers interested in becoming mentors.

From the literature, three lists of items that might be helpful in the mentoring of first-year teachers were developed. They focused upon characteristics of mentors, activities of mentoring, and elements of organizational structure. How these items were developed into final compilations will be explained later.

Method

In an attempt to begin to reach a consensus regarding elements helpful in the mentoring of first-year teachers, a modified form of the Delphi Technique was used. Basically, the method used involved five steps:

1. A three-part questionnaire composed of characteristics, activities, and elements of organizational structure was developed from the literature on mentoring.

2. The questionnaire was sent to 164 mentors to obtain their reactions, based on their experience, and to allow them to add items that they felt were missing from the questionnaire.

3. A second questionnaire was developed from the responses to Round I and sent to respondents asking them to rate, based on their expertise, each of the eighty-eight items in terms of the item's helpfulness in mentoring in general.

4. A third questionnaire was developed from the results of the responses to Round II and was mailed to respondents asking them to reconsider their response to each item in relation to the group response to each item and, in some cases, a sample rationale given by a mentor.

5. The responses to the final round were analyzed to form the output of the study.

Subjects

The modified Delphi Technique provided a reasonable method for gathering the judgments of all 164 experienced mentors who had participated in New York State's Mentor Teacher-Internship Program during the 1987–1988 school year. The study attempted to use the entire group of available mentors from that year. Participation in the study was voluntary.

Taken as a group, the subjects represented twenty-eight of the twenty-nine projects funded by New York State during 1987–1988. These mentors were considered experts based on the following criteria.

1. They were experienced mentors.

2. They had volunteered to be mentors.

3. They were selected by their local project committee to serve as mentors.

4. They were judged by their project's selection committee to meet the criteria established by the state. Those criteria were (a) permanently certified, (b) demonstrated mastery of pedagogical and subject matter skills, (c) superior teaching abilities, (d) interpersonal relationship qualities, and (e) indicated willingness to participate.

Collectively, the group of mentors could be described by the following demographic data:

1. More than 70 percent were female.

2. A majority (60 percent) were between the ages of 36 and 45.

3. More than half were graduates of state colleges.

4. Nearly 75 percent held undergraduate degrees in education.

5. Seventy-five percent held a master's degree.

Conducting the Study

Round I

In September 1988, the Round I questionnaire and a cover letter outlining the design of the study were mailed to all 164 mentors who were part of the New York State Mentor Teacher-Internship Program (NYS MTIP) Evaluation Study during the 1987–1988 school year. Participants were asked to complete the form and return it within ten days. Ninety-eight of the original 164 questionnaires (approximately 60 percent) were received within the time limit.

Round II

The results from Round I were tallied and used to develop the questionnaire for Round II. Based on the suggestions of the mentors, additional items were added to the original lists in each section of the questionnaire. The second round instrument was reorganized to reflect the first round responses and refocused from the experience of the mentors to their expertise. In Round II, the mentors were asked to shift their perspective and to consider each item as it would be helpful to mentoring in general in an ideal context. Mentors were asked to judge each item even if it had not been a part of their personal experiences.

Participants in the second round were asked to rate the helpfulness of each item using a nine-point Likert scale.

Items on the rating scale were labeled as follows:

Least Helpful   Moderately Helpful   Most Helpful
  1 2 3   4 5 6   7 8 9

An item judged to be least helpful would be indicated by circling one, two, or three depending on how intensely the mentor felt about that particular item. In similar fashion, a rating of four, five, or six would indicate that the mentor judged an item to be moderately helpful; while a seven, eight, or nine would indicate an item to be most helpful to the mentor. It was though that nine-point scale would allow for a sufficient range of responses.

At the end of each section of the questionnaire, mentors were asked to select the two items they rated the highest and to explain their thinking related to the helpfulness of each of those items.

Ninety-eight questionnaires were mailed in mid-October. Sixty-five responses were returned. This represented approximately 66 percent of those mailed; and approximately 40 percent of the original mailing.

Responses were systematically organized by item and analyzed to produce a group mean and standard deviation for each item. Items were then placed in descending order by group means within each section of the questionnaire. Representative rationale statements were also included in the questionnaire for Round III.

Round III

The final questionnaire provided each participant with (a) the items from Round II reorganized in descending order based on the group means; (b) the group mean for each item; (c) the standard deviation for each item; (d) the individual's response (1 to 9) to each item from Round II; (e) if available from Round II, sample rationale statements relating a participant's reasons for judging an item to be helpful; and (f) the same scale (1 to 9) for rating each item a final time.

Respondents were asked to provide a final rating for each item on the third questionnaire after they had considered the information provided from other respondents. If participants' responses to a particular item in Round II had been more than one standard deviation from the mean, the mentors were asked to consider their responses in light of its relationship to the group. If participants chose not to change their responses, they were asked to explain their rationale for their position.

Forty-eight of the sixty-five questionnaires mailed in November were returned. This represented approximately 74 percent of the questionnaires mailed for Round III; and approximately 30 percent of the original mailing.

Responses to Round III were analyzed to determine group mean and standard deviation in order to compare these responses to those obtained in Round II. The responses to the final questionnaire were reordered to represent the degree to which the participants of this study judged each item to be helpful to the mentoring of first-year teachers. The results of these three rounds and their content were analyzed and summarized to produce the results of this study.

Presentation of Data

The purpose of this study was to collect and organize the judgements of experienced mentors regarding elements that are helpful in the mentoring of first-year teachers. Participants in this study did rate certain elements to be more helpful than others.

Characteristics of Mentors

The first section of the study dealt with personal and professional characteristics of mentors. In Round I, most of the characteristics taken from the literature on mentoring were judged to be helpful. As the study progressed, participants did indicate that some characteristics of mentors were more helpful than others. Table 8.1 presents the results of Round I and Round II of this part of the study.

Table 8.1

Characteristics of Mentors

Comparison of the Results from Rounds II and III

Means ($\overline{X}$) and standard deviations (sd) from Rounds II and III.

		RII		RIII	
Order*	Item	$\overline{X}$	(sd)	$\overline{X}$	(sd)
1.	approachability	8.4	(0.9)	8.7	(0.5)
2.	integrity	8.4	(1.0)	8.6	(0.8)
3.	good listener	8.3	(1.0)	8.5	(0.7)
4.	sincerity	8.1	(1.0)	8.4	(0.8)
5.	willingness to spend time	8.1	(1.0)	8.4	(0.8)
6.	enthusiasm	8.2	(1.0)	8.3	(0.8)
7.	**teaching competence****	8.2	(1.1)	8.3	(0.8)
8.	trust	8.1	(1.2)	8.3	(0.9)
9.	receptivity	8.1	(1.2)	8.3	(0.7)
10.	willingness to work hard	8.1	(1.1)	8.3	(0.8)
11.	positive outlook	8.0	(1.1)	8.2	(0.8)
12.	confidence	7.8	(1.4)	8.2	(0.9)
13.	commitment to profession	8.1	(1.1)	8.2	(0.8)
14.	openness	7.9	(1.0)	8.1	(0.7)
15.	**experience in teaching**	7.7	(1.4)	8.1	(0.8)
16.	tactfulness	7.8	(1.3)	8.0	(1.0)
17.	cooperativeness	8.0	(0.9)	8.0	(0.7)
18.	flexibility	7.9	(1.4)	8.0	(1.0)
19.	concern	7.9	(1.1)	7.9	(1.0)
20.	sense of humor	7.6	(1.4)	7.8	(1.1)
21.	**organization**	7.7	(1.2)	7.8	(1.0)
22.	**patience**	7.6	(1.2)	7.6	(0.9)
23.	**empathy**	7.3	(1.5)	7.6	(1.0)
24.	initiative	7.6	(1.4)	7.6	(1.6)
25.	**reflectiveness on how people learn**	7.5	(1.3)	7.5	(0.9)
26.	**consciously skilled**	7.4	(1.4)	7.5	(0.8)
27.	ability to take criticism	7.5	(1.2)	7.5	(1.0)
28.	candidness	7.1	(1.4)	7.4	(1.0)
29.	**unselfishness**	7.1	(1.5)	7.3	(1.0)
30.	intelligence	7.2	(1.3)	7.3	(1.0)
31.	**well educated**	7.0	(1.5)	7.2	(0.9)
32.	**determination**	7.2	(1.4)	7.1	(0.9)
33.	**knowledgeable about district**	7.1	(1.6)	7.1	(1.2)
34.	autonomy	6.8	(1.8)	6.8	(1.2)
35.	**knowledge of current research**	6.6	(1.7)	6.6	(0.4)
36.	**humility**	6.5	(1.7)	6.6	(1.3)

Round II (N = 65)

Round III (N = 48)

*Characteristics were placed in descending order according to the group means from Round III.

**Boldfaced type indicates the characteristics that were added by participants in Round I.

Experienced mentors, drawing on their expertise, considered all the identified characteristics of mentors moderately to very helpful, but some to be more helpful than others.

Perhaps of greater significance is the degree of consensus represented by the standard deviations. Twenty-one of the characteristics had a standard deviation of less than one. Only five items—initiative, knowledgeable about the district, autonomy, knowledge of current research, and humility—had standard deviations of 1.2 or greater.

In Round II, several respondents included explanations for their ratings of particular items in the study. Taken together, these comments can be categorized in the following manner:

1. They refer to who the mentor is as a professional. Members of the panel expressed conviction that in order to be successful, it would be helpful if a mentor were competent, committed to the profession, experienced, consciously skilled, and knowledgeable about teaching, learning, and the district in which she works. One mentor wrote, "We need to be aware of what we do that works and why [it works]."

2. Other comments refer to who the mentor is as a person. It was suggested that mentors may be more successful if they were approachable, of high integrity, a good listener, sincere, and cooperative. Panelists noted, "If you and the intern can't be candid with each other, what is the purpose of trust and respect?" Others noted the need for determination, patience, initiative, and empathy. One mentor wrote, "I remember what it was like the first years and who helped me."

3. Many of the explanations indicated that panelists saw some items in the study as being related to both personal and professional characteristics. A few of these items were enthusiasm, organization, and initiative. One comment pointed out that a mentor needed to be well organized, both personally and professionally, "just to have the time necessary to accomplish everything that needs to be done."

Considered together, the quantitative and qualitative results of this study demonstrate that (a) respondents did reconsider some of their ratings, (b) movement toward consensus did occur, and (c) individual mentors held strong views of the helpfulness of some characteristics of mentors.

Activities of Mentoring

The second focus of this study was the activities of mentoring. The original list, developed from the literature, was divided into activities engaged in with the intern or activities that might have involved the mentor or intern but not both. Table 8.2 presents the results of the participants' ratings of the activities done with the intern.

Panelists expressed their belief that encouraging, counseling, and modeling were among the most helpful activities participated in with the intern. Also highly rated was having informal discussions. It was noted that, "Friendship and informal discussions seem to affect the entire team's productivity." The elements of interpersonal relationships were judged to be very helpful because they created a foundation for "the professional give and take which develops over time with colleagues."

If the ratings for having informal discussions (8.0) and holding routine formal discussions (6.4) are compared, then it seems clear that the panelists in this study judged informal discussions to be more helpful. One mentor noted, "Immediate feedback seems more valuable."

Other Activities

Table 8.3 presents a comparison of the results from Round II and Round III that dealt with activities that were not done together.

Participants noted that it was of great importance to provide mentor training programs that assisted them in preparing for their new roles as mentors. The helpfulness of having the intern observe other teachers was also an activity upon which there was a reasonable degree of consensus. Many of the other activities (meeting with other mentors, mentor attending workshops and seminars, informal

Table 8.2
Activities with the Intern
Comparison of the Results from Rounds II and III
Means ($\overline{X}$) and standard deviation (sd) from Rounds II and III

Order*	Activity	RII		RIII	
		$\overline{X}$	*(sd)*	$\overline{X}$	*(sd)*
1.	encouraging	7.9	(1.4)	8.2	(0.9)
2.	counseling	7.7	(1.5)	8.1	(1.1)
3.	modeling	7.4	(1.4)	8.1	(1.2)
4.	having informal discussions	8.0	(1.0)	8.0	(0.8)
5.	mentor observing intern	7.6	(1.2)	7.4	(0.8)
6.	**orienting intern to staff** **and district****	7.1	(1.7)	7.4	(1.1)
7.	intern observing mentor	7.4	(1.6)	7.4	(1.3)
8.	befriending	7.1	(1.6)	7.0	(1.4)
9.	participating in workshops and seminars	6.8	(1.8)	6.9	(1.6)
10.	joint planning	6.9	(1.6)	6.8	(1.2)
11.	reviewing materials for teaching	6.8	(1.4)	6.8	(1.2)
12.	**attending conferences together**	6.6	(2.0)	6.7	(1.7)
13.	holding routine formal discussions	6.1	(2.0)	6.4	(1.5)
14.	teaching together	6.6	(1.9)	6.4	(1.5)
15.	teaching the intern	6.0	(2.0)	6.0	(1.4)
16.	**social events**	4.7	(2.0)	4.6	(1.7)

Round II (N = 65)
Round III (N = 48)
*Activities were placed in descending order according to the group means from Round III.
**Boldfaced type indicates the activities that were added by participants in Round I.

meetings with other mentors, mentor visiting other schools, reading about mentoring, and mentor sharing at faculty meetings) point to ways of increasing knowledge of the process of mentoring both for mentors and other faculty who may serve as mentors in the future.

Seven respondents wrote more general comments that referred to two or more activities. These comments fell into three categories:

1. Supporting the overall value of more than one of the activities. For example, "The mentor needs as much help as possible—these activities (attending workshops and seminars, and mentor visiting other schools) provide those needs."

Table 8.3

Other Activities

Comparison of the Results from Rounds II and III

Means ($\overline{X}$) and standard deviation (sd) from Rounds II and III.

		RII		RIII	
Order*	Activity	$\overline{X}$	(sd)	$\overline{X}$	(sd)
1.	**mentor training program****	7.6	(1.4)	7.8	(0.9)
2.	intern observing other teachers	7.6	(1.5)	7.7	(1.2)
3.	meeting with other mentors	7.3	(2.2)	6.9	(1.7)
4.	mentor attending workshops and seminars	6.7	(2.0)	6.9	(1.7)
5.	**informal meetings with other mentors**	6.7	(1.8)	6.8	(1.4)
6.	sponsoring the intern	6.4	(2.0)	6.7	(1.5)
7.	attending state or regional conferences	6.4	(2.0)	6.4	(1.7)
8.	mentor visiting other schools	6.1	(2.0)	6.4	(1.6)
9.	**reading about mentoring**	5.9	(2.0)	6.1	(1.4)
10.	**mentor sharing at faculty meetings**	5.6	(2.1)	5.8	(1.4)
11.	attending national conferences	5.6	(2.1)	5.8	(1.8)

Round II (N = 65)

Round III (N = 48)

*The activities were arranged in descending order according to the mean from Round III.

**Boldfaced type indicates the activities that were added by participants in Round I.

2. Comparing these activities to other things that had been considered. For example, "I don't think any of the activities on this page are nearly as important to a successful program as 'activities with the mentor' or 'characteristics of mentors'."

3. Contrasting their program or individual situation. For example, (his project) "may be unique—my teaching load and responsibilities to my four interns takes most of my time. I attend state conferences and often get 'sucked into' discussions of mentoring as part of (his district's) reform efforts."

It is interesting to note the variety of responses received for mentor visiting other schools, attending state or regional conferences, attending national conferences, and mentor sharing at faculty meetings.

The comments help to illustrate the diversity of opinions held by mentors regarding these items. Although movement toward consensus was indicated by the change in means and standard deviations, these comments clearly indicated that there is still substantial difference of views among the participants of this study.

The data collected in this part of this study suggests that the participants generally believe these activities to be helpful to the mentoring of first-year teachers. However, considerable differences of opinion were observed among participants who wrote to share their rationales for their ratings of particular items. This might suggest that these activities need to be carefully considered within the particular set of contexts of each project and for each mentor-intern relationship.

Organizational Structure

The third section of this study dealt with elements of organizational structure that were helpful to the mentoring of first-year teachers. These elements were divided into two lists: elements of overall project structure,and elements of project support for the mentor.

Table 8.4 presents a comparison of the results of Round II and Round III related to elements of overall project structure.

Comments related to these elements of overall project structure included the following notes:

1. Clearly defined roles for participants: "No—Each situation must develop its own role to suit a variety of needs."

2. Roles for previous mentors and interns: "The experiences and expertise of those that went through the process would benefit people new to the program."

3. Clear roles for principals and supervisors: We need to "make distinction between support and evaluation."

4. Effective project introduction to school community: "Not all interns have their own classes—mine was the GAT [Gifted and Talented Students] teacher—both her job and

Table 8.4
Elements of Overall Project Structure
Comparison of the Results of Rounds II and III
Means ($\overline{X}$) and standard deviations (sd) from Rounds II and III.

		RII		RIII	
Order*	Element	$\overline{X}$	(sd)	$\overline{X}$	(sd)
1.	effective preplanning for the project	7.8	(1.5)	8.1	(1.0)
2.	**administrative support for the project****	7.7	(1.9)	8.0	(1.5)
3.	effective matching of mentors and interns	7.8	(1.4)	7.9	(1.3)
4.	**clearly defined roles for participants**	7.7	(1.6)	7.9	(1.2)
5.	cooperation by teachers and administrators	7.3	(1.8)	7.7	(1.3)
6.	leadership from project coordinators	7.1	(2.0)	7.6	(1.1)
7.	clear roles from principals and supervisors	6.8	(2.2)	7.4	(1.3)
8.	**roles for previous mentors and interns**	7.1	(1.8)	7.2	(1.4)
9.	effective project introduction into the community	6.5	(2.2)	6.9	(1.4)
10.	use of consultants	6.4	(1.8)	6.7	(1.4)
11.	yearlong steering committee	6.2	(1.8)	6.6	(1.1)

Round II (N = 65)
Round III (N = 48)
*Elements were placed in descending order according to the group means from Round III.
**Boldfaced type indicates the elements that were added by participants in Round I.

her status as an intern needed to be explained and accepted to create the proper atmosphere for her progress."

5. Use of consultants: "We use consultants to train both the mentors and the interns in Staff Development situations, particularly in interpersonal relations. We also include mentor trainees who will replace the present mentors/hopefully better prepared."

6. Yearlong steering committee: "It's extremely important for representatives from all involved groups (interns,

mentors, union, administrators, etc.) to be actively involved and meet throughout the year to discuss what is working with the program and what needs to be ironed out."

In table 8.4, data is displayed that suggests the importance associated with effective preplanning, administrative and faculty support, and clearly defined roles for all those directly or indirectly involved in mentoring programs.

Project Support for the Mentor

The last section of the study asked participants to consider elements of project support for the mentor. Table 8.5 presents the results of this section.

In sharing their thinking about items in table 8.5, participants showed strong consensus on the helpfulness of adequate release time, orientation for the mentors, and satisfactory substitute arrangements. These are items that can enhance the mentoring process or, if poorly done, cause a great deal of hardship. Mentors are concerned that they be provided with adequate support and training. They want to be successful. Table 8.5 provides food for thought as to how we can structure projects to provide sufficient, productive support to enable them to succeed.

Discussion of the Data

The results of this study suggest that the individual characteristics of mentors are helpful in the process of mentoring. Mentors indicated that most of the items identified from the literature had been helpful in their experiences. Overall, eighteen of the thirty-six characteristics of mentors received a mean rating of 8.0 or higher. Two characteristics of mentors, approachability and integrity, were the highest rated of all eighty-eight items in the study. The mentors have made it clear that the characteristics of mentors are helpful to mentoring. Policy-

Table 8.5

Elements of Project Support for Mentors
Comparison of the Results of Rounds II and III
Means ($\overline{X}$) and standard deviations (sd) from Rounds II and III

		RII		RIII	
Order*	Element	$\overline{X}$	(sd)	$\overline{X}$	(sd)
1.	adequate release time	8.1	(1.7)	8.5	(0.7)
2.	orientation for the mentors	8.1	(1.4)	8.4	(0.7)
3.	satisfactory substitute arrangements	7.9	(1.9)	8.3	(1.2)
4.	**union support****	7.2	(1.9)	7.8	(1.2)
5.	joint meetings with other mentors	7.4	(1.6)	7.7	(1.2)
6.	**availability of project leaders**	7.3	(1.8)	7.7	(1.0)
7.	**informal networks with other mentors**	7.1	(1.9)	7.5	(1.1)
8.	seminars on mentoring	7.2	(1.9)	7.5	(1.6)
9.	**acceptance of other teachers**	7.2	(1.5)	7.4	(1.1)
10.	sufficient materials on mentoring	7.1	(1.7)	7.1	(1.3)
11.	attendance at conferences	6.5	(1.9)	6.6	(1.6)
12.	networks with other projects in area	6.2	(2.1)	6.3	(1.7)
13.	mentors received special recognition	5.5	(2.3)	5.7	(1.9)
14.	preferred treatment in materials order	4.7	(2.2)	4.7	(2.0)

Round II (N = 65)
Round III (N = 48)
*The elements were arranged in descending order according to the mean from Round III.
**Boldfaced type indicates the elements that were added by participants in Round I.

makers, researchers, and project planners are encouraged to consider that who the mentor is, both personally and professionally, will be a paramount concern for any mentoring project.

Encouraging, counseling, modeling, having informal discussion, and mentor training programs are activities rated as being most helpful by the participants of this study. Further, data gathered in this study suggest that holding formal discussions and teaching together were not part of the experiences of many mentors. Mentors did not rate activities engaged in without the intern as highly as activities done with the intern. Perhaps project planners need to consider the desirability of planning for a "flexible" project which would allow for more informal opportunities for mentors and interns.

The diversity of projects involved in the NYS MTI Program was evident in the results of this study regarding the elements of organizational structure. Mentors stressed the helpfulness of adequate release time, orientation for the mentors, and satisfactory substitute arrangements. These data help to point out some of the considerations that might be made in planning mentoring projects in the future. Mentor projects might be well served by a cautious approach to formal planning. The results of this study suggest that it would be helpful if a mentoring project placed emphasis on providing adequate release time, orientation for the mentors, and satisfactory substitute arrangements while allowing for flexibility in how the mentor and intern allocate their time. Structure and flexibility need not be mutually exclusive.

Mentors have judged personal characteristics such as approachability, integrity, active listening, and sincerity as being very helpful to the process of mentoring. Experienced mentors have noted that professional characteristics like willingness to spend time, teaching competence, commitment to the profession, and experience in teaching are also very helpful.

Mentors need to be professional teachers who are knowledgeable about pedagogy and who possess excellent interpersonal skills in working with adults. Certainly, this is an extremely complex issue. It is not an easy task to access a prospective mentor in light of such characteristics. Indeed it may seem that this is advocating that only "super" people can or will be successful mentors. This is not the case. However, the results of this study indicate that it may be worthwhile to be extremely careful in the selection of mentor teachers.

Experienced mentors reported their beliefs that the personal and professional characteristics of mentors are critical contributing factors to the success or failure of the process of mentoring. This is not surprising given the importance of the relationship between the mentor and the new teacher. As people, we take our personal characteristics into new relationships. Those relationships are affected by who we are.

Mentors do not work in isolation. The results of this study indicate that mentors can be helped by support from their colleagues, administrators, unions or associations, and the other members of the school community.

Mentors, and those who support them, must be ready to deal with difficult issues of equity. Problems may emerge whenever change involving special status or scheduling is introduced into the culture of a school. Other teachers may resent or envy the new mentor. These issues have been faced by some mentors.

At the heart of New York State's view of mentoring is the relationship between the mentor and the new teacher. This relationship is complex and unique. It exists within the contexts of a specific school in a specific community. Each school must recognize the uniqueness of its set of circumstances as it conceptualizes, develops, supports, and evaluates its own mentoring project. It may be best to begin with the realization that projects cannot be borrowed from other schools. Each school must develop its own plan in light of its needs and resources. However, in the process of so doing, educators can benefit by the experience of teachers who have been pioneers in serving as mentors to new teachers.

Summary

This study attempted to seek consensus among experienced mentors regarding what elements are helpful in the mentoring of first-year teachers. A modified form of the Delphi-Technique involving a reiteration of questionnaires was used to gather data from the population of 164 mentors who had been part of the NYS MTI Program in 1987–1988. The results of this study suggest that policymakers, researchers, prospective mentors, administrators, and project planners would be well served to consider the following points:

1. The personal and professional characteristics of mentors are helpful to successful mentoring.

2. Many of the characteristics included in this study are learned behaviors. Therefore, they may be able to be taught, developed, or enhanced in teachers before they assume the new role of mentor.

3. Mentor projects should employ a cautious approach to formal structure. They should be sensitive to the need for flexibility according to each school's specific context. Mentors have indicated that informal sessions may be more helpful than rigid, formal blocks of time. There may even be a need to adjust the amount of time available to the mentor and intern over the course of the year.

Project planners might use the results of this study, as represented by the five tables included in this chapter, as a framework for considering questions to be dealt with as they plan to select mentors (table 8.1), allow for activities of mentoring (tables 8.2 and 8.3), design their overall project structure (table 8.4), and provide support for the mentors (table 8.5).

Mentoring holds hope for improving the first year of teaching, and therefore, the induction into teaching process. Like the analogy of being "new" at helping someone learn to drive, those involved in mentoring can benefit from the experiences of those who have assumed these new roles before us. Project planners stand to benefit from the suggestions made by experienced mentors.

Note

Panelists

This list presents forty of the forty-eight panelists who contributed to each of the three rounds of this study. Those listed granted their permission to include their names in this study. The wishes of the eight who did not desire to have their names included have been respected. A special admiration and gratitude is felt for each mentor whose reflections made this study possible.

Linda Barbato	Jean Hakinian
James C. Boardman	Patricia Jones
Ruth B. Bonn	Deborah Leff
Joan Brown	William Lutz
N. J. Cenerilli	Anne Mielenhausen
Marilyn Compo	Connie M. Miller
John Cosgriff	Jamie Moessel
Jonetta Darcy	Carl E. O'Connell
Barbara Davis	John D. Parry
Jacquelyn Dawson	John Pelkey
Marcia DeFran	Karene Person
Rosalyn Della Pietra	Johanna Peterson
John Donovan	Marianne J. Schaffner
Mary N. Drachler	Gloria Sena
Terri Drossos	Gerald T. Sherman
Mildred Farinella	Daphine Somerville
Diane L. Fortman	Al Stevens
Rosemary B. Frenyea	Marilyn Stuzin
Joan Grossman	Constance M. Wang
Sam Hammond	Jeanne Wells

References

Anderson, E.; and Shannon, A. (1988). Toward a conceptualization of mentoring. *Journal of Teacher Education, 39*(1), 38–42.

Egan, J. (1985). *A descriptive study of classroom teacher's mentor-protege roles and relationships.* Unpublished doctoral dissertation, Syracuse University, Syracuse, NY.

Galvez-Hjornevik, C. (1986). Mentoring among teachers: A review of the literature. *Journal of Teacher Education, 37* (1), 6–11.

Gehrke, N.; and Kay, R. (1984). The socialization of beginning teachers through mentor-protege relationships. *Journal of Teacher Education, 35*(3), 21–24.

Gray, W.; and Gray, M. (1985). Synthesis of research on mentoring beginning teachers. *Educational Leadership, 43*(3), 37–43.

Hoffman, J.; Edwards, S.; O'Neil, S.; Barnes, S.; and Paulissen, M. (1986). A study of state-mandated beginning teacher programs. *Journal of Teacher Education*, 38(1), 16–21.

Mager, G. (1986). *Support for first-year teachers: New York State's mentor teacher-internship program.* Unpublished manuscript.

Reinhartz, J., ed. (1989). *Teacher induction.* Washington, DC: National Education Association.

Ryan, K.; Newman, K.; Mager, G.; Applegate, J.; Lasley, T.; Flora, R.; and Johnson, J. (1980). *Biting the apple: Accounts of first-year teachers.* New York: Longman.

Showers, B. (1984). Peer coaching and its affects on transfer of training. Paper presented at the annual meeting of the American Educational Research Association, New Orleans, LA.

Thies-Sprinthall, L. (1986). A collaborative approach for mentor training: A working model. *Journal of Teacher Education,* 37(6), 13–20.

Veenman, S. (1984). Perceived problems of beginning teachers. *Review of Educational Research, 54*(1), 143–178.

9. Lessons and Questions from School-Based Collaborative Programs

GARY P. DEBOLT

This chapter ties together common themes, features, and questions raised by those preceding it. You the reader are encouraged to reflect upon what can be learned from reports of collaborative school-based programs to support new teachers. Theory and practice can inform each other.

This volume has attempted to examine the place of induction in the ever-changing process of becoming a teacher. In chapter 1, Mager analyzed the place of induction in this process of becoming a teacher. He has suggested that it is helpful to think of becoming a teacher as:

> the continuous experience of an individual through which an image of self-as-teacher is formed and refined, and during which knowledge, skills, and values appropriate to the work of teaching, as it is to be practiced in a particular context, are acquired and used (p. 6).

In this light, the process of induction into teaching and the use of experienced, successful classroom teachers to serve as mentors of new teachers has been examined.

In reflecting upon the place of mentoring in the process of induction, one is struck by the complexity of teaching in schools today and the multitude of roles and activities that may be required to be a successful mentor. We, as educators, are working toward a clear understanding of what it means to be a mentor and what this entails.

To this complex issue, we add the questions and issues that accompany attempts to formalize and systematize the mentoring process and relationships. The nature of most schools makes it difficult, at best, for mentoring relationships to occur naturally, whereby the new teacher selects a mentor based on his or her own set of criteria and needs. Instead, formal programs attempt to assign mentors to new teachers. Is this the only way we can proceed?

In the second part of this volume, five school-based collaborative mentoring programs were reported. Similar aspects of these programs may serve to focus our thinking about the usefulness of these reports to us. Allow us to consider their goals, training of mentors, and identified strengths and benefits of each program.

Goals

In order to consider the goals and objectives of these programs, a chart might be helpful. Each project is concerned with providing support and assistance for new teachers. The stated goals reflect the desire to ease the pressures on the first-year teacher. It is interesting to note that there are some differences in goals. For instance, the New Mexico/Albuquerque Project specifies its desire to provide professional development for experienced teachers and to develop collaboration between public schools and higher education. These two goals are very important. Although they were not explicitly stated by the other projects, it might be inferred that these are of common concern. The professional development of experienced teachers is an essential benefit of mentoring projects. Research dealing with mentors' experiences has shown the benefits which accrue to mentors (McKenna 1988, DeBolt 1989). Collaboration between public schools and institutions of higher education is an issue of increasing importance. Certainly, all of the projects represent collaborative efforts which have the potential for positive outcomes.

Another goal of note is to increase the numbers of African American and Hispanic teachers in the New York City schools. Hunter College has a long history of collaborative work with School #4 in East Harlem. Together, they are attempting to address a major issue in teacher development. Their concern is not only the recruitment of African-American and Hispanic teachers, but also the retention of

Figure 9.1
Goals

UNM/Albuquerque	North Country Consortium	ASU/Maricopa Schools	Hunter College/ East Harlem Schools	UNC/Local Schools
1. guidance for new teachers • analysis and reflection on teaching through coaching • foundation to become self-reliant 2. assistance for new teachers 3. professional development for experienced teachers 4. collaboration between public schools and higher education	1. to improve performance of new teachers 2. to enhance retention 3. maximize the use of resources 4. develop regional decision-making organization	1. immediate and ongoing instructional guidance for new teachers 2. personal support for new teachers	1. academic and personal-social support for new teachers 2. greater understanding of the needs of new teachers 3. increase the numbers of African-American and Puerto Rican teachers	1. to provide a safe environment for new teachers 2. to have the support personnel adjust to the needs of individual new teachers as the year progresses 3. allow for problem solving and decision making

those teachers. They seek this goal through supporting and striving to understand the needs of these individual new teachers.

The desire to maximize the use of resources, stated by the North Country Consortium, is also important. Maximization of resource use is an interesting goal. It is a very timely issue, especially in a widespread, often isolated, rural area. Schools need to find ways to share resources, both financial and human.

Two projects, the North Country Consortium and the University of Northern Colorado, both expressed the desire to provide for decision making and problem solving. This may be a reflection of the move toward shared decision making.

Training of Mentors

The training of participants is an important feature of support programs. Concern for the needs of new teachers is appropriate. It is also worthwhile to consider the transition being made by an experienced teacher who is mentoring for the first time. Working to support an adult colleague is very different from teaching children. Preparation for this new role is essential, helpful, and desired by mentors (DeBolt 1989).

Training and preparing the mentors for their new roles is important in each program. Although the format selected for the training may differ, the content is strikingly similar. All of the programs emphasize skills and knowledge needed by mentors such as observation and conferencing skills, stages of adult development, and effective teaching practices. Individual projects also note special emphasis: fostering self-esteem (UNM), district organization and staff development (North Country), the Arizona Teacher Residency Instrument (ASU), getting along with administrators (Hunter) and relationships among mentors, principals, and field consultants (UNC). Each emphasis reveals an area of special need or concern to that project. Others involved in mentoring might benefit from examining the specific reports of those projects that have reported elements of special interest to them.

Figure 9.2
Training of Mentors

UNM/Albuquerque	North Country Consortium	ASU/Maricopa Schools	Hunter College/East Harlem Schools	UNC/Local Schools
Weekly Seminars	Summer Training	Workshops	Workshops	In-house Training/Orientation
1. rationale	1. dimensions of mentor's roles	1. assessment and clinical supervision	1. building trust	1. program expectations
2. stages of teacher development	2. stages of teacher growth	2. Arizona Teacher Residency Instrument	2. role of the mentor	2. descriptions of roles and responsibilities
3. concerns of beginning teachers	3. adult development and learning	• teaching plans and materials	3. identifying and solving problems	3. induction
4. fostering self-esteem	4. district organization and staff development	• classroom procedures	4. developing communication skills	4. support behaviors
5. working with adults	5. group encounters	• interpersonal skills	5. offering constructive criticism	5. relationships among mentor, principal, and field consultant
6. teacher mentoring	6. effective teaching skills	3. effective teacher behaviors	6. dealing with disruptive children	6. analysis of instruction
7. classroom observation and conferencing skills	7. counseling skills	4. coaching	7. transitions	7. conferencing
8. teacher reflection	8. peer coaching	5. conferencing	8. writing lesson plans	8. feedback
9. teacher coaching	9. interactive supervisor	6. focused observation	9. getting along with administrators	9. optional graduate seminar
	10. teaching and learning styles		10. communicating with parents	10. management
	11. management			11. communication
	12. curriculum development			

Figure 9.3
Strengths and Benefits

UNM/Albuquerque	North Country Consortium	ASU/Maricopa Schools	Hunter College/East Harlem Schools	UNC/Local Schools
• selection of mentors	• documented evaluation	• can be extended to second or third year of teaching	• support for beginning minority teachers for first three years	• support for new teachers and reentry individual (nontraditional)
• collaboration	• new teachers' growth	• evaluation based on instrument	• collaboration	• holistic teacher
• new teachers	• mentors' growth	• ongoing research to gather data for analysis and reflection	• trust	• support team
• professional growth	• school district	• effectiveness of training	• "history" of working together	• 85 percent retention for following year
• positive attitudes	• formalized support	• improvement of new teachers' performance	• communication	
• focused instruction	• replacement (sub) teacher training	• satisfaction	• confidentiality	
• mentors	• consortium	• perception of mentor's functions	• shared responsibility	
• confidence	• improved use of resources	• communication between mentors and new teachers	• 98 percent retention over three years	
• perspectives	• flexibility			
• communication				
• principals				
• "multiplier effect"				
• district				
• progress				
• communication—				
• retention—				

Strengths and Benefits

Researchers have reported strengths and benefits that have been observed in each program. Each of the five programs presented here emphasize certain perceived strengths and benefits. A connection can be seen between the stated goals of each program (figure 9.1) and the reported strengths. For example, Hunter College's program expressly set out to improve the retention rate of teachers from minority groups. They report a 98 percent retention over a three-year period. UNM and UNC also report very impressive retention rates (85 percent). The North Country Group reports improved use of resources and flexibility as positive outcomes of their consortium's efforts to support new teachers. Overall, the projects document positive effects of their efforts as they relate to the new teachers. This is a forward step in efforts to improve the induction into teaching process.

Conclusion

From this brief examination of five reported programs several issues emerge.

1. Collaboration between public schools and institutions of higher education is extremely beneficial and desirable.

2. The need to support new teachers may be even more critical today in light of increased demands and pressures affecting teaching.

3. Support of teachers from minority groups is especially necessary as we prepare to deal with the changing demographics of our nation's schools.

4. Mentoring programs need to include context specific training and ongoing support.

5. Positive benefits can be accrued by the collaborating agencies and the individuals involved in these programs.

The reports of these programs also suggest some additional issues for consideration.

1. Odell and Ferarro note that new teachers don't have to be taken out of the classroom to be supported.

2. Replacement teachers (substitutes) are an integral part of any program that takes the mentor or the new teacher out of his or her classroom. Stupiansky and Wolfe believe that replacement teachers also need to be trained and treated as part of the instructional team.

3. According to Taharally, and Enz et al, specific situations may dictate that induction support programs continue to provide support into the second and third years.

4. "Assistance is more effective than assessment." as noted by Jacobsen.

5. Jacobsen further suggests that we might benefit by providing support to the person who is reentering the teaching profession after a long hiatus.

There are still many unanswered questions that deal specifically with mentoring and more generally with the larger context.

1. Can anyone be a mentor?

2. What will be the fate of educational reforms, such as mentoring, in the economic hard times now being seen in several states?

3. Can we find creative ways to support mentoring without additional cost? Is money always the answer?

4. As schools change, how can (or should) mentors and mentoring change? Should these changes be at a local, state, or national level?

5. Should there be national standards for mentors?

6. Would having a poor mentor be worse than not having a mentor at all?

7. Should we be trying to develop more informal programs for mentors, or is that an oxymoron?

8. Is it more critical to provide mentor training in content mastery, pedagogy, of interpersonal skills? Does it matter?

9. Can we learn from research reports based on the experience of teachers who have been mentors?

Nathalie J. Gehrke, in her article "Seeing Our Way to Better Helping of Beginning Teachers" (1991), has suggested that educators might do well to look beyond education to some of the social sciences. From the social sciences more might be learned about beginners and beginnings in general. She makes an interesting argument for the need to replace shortsighted helping programs with programs to develop schools as helping communities.

The programs discussed in this book have shown many important issues that need to be considered in examining or designing mentoring projects. Much can be learned by their reports and the questions they raise. Mentoring offers great hope toward the goal of improving the induction into teaching process.

It seems reasonable to conclude that it would be in the best interest of improved induction and instruction to look for ways to make schools places of pervasive caring for teachers as well as for students.

References

DeBolt, G. (1989). *Helpful elements in the mentoring of first-year teachers.* Unpublished dissertation. Syracuse, NY: Syracuse University.

DeBolt, G. (Ed.) (In press). *Teacher induction and mentoring: School-based collaborative programs.* Albany, NY: SUNY Press.

Enz, B.; Anderson, G.; Weber, B.; and Lawhead, D. (In press). The Arizona Teacher Residency Program. In G. DeBolt, ed., *Teacher induction and mentoring: School-based collaborative programs.* Albany, NY: SUNY Press.

Gehrke, N. (1991). Seeing our way to better helping of beginning teachers. *The Educational Forum, 55*(3), 233–242.

Huling-Austin, L.; Odell, S.; Ishler, P.; Kay, R.; and Edelfelt, R. (1989). *Assisting the beginning teacher.* Reston, VA: Association of Teacher Educators.

Jacobsen, M. (In press). Mentoring as a university/public school partnership. In G. DeBolt, ed., *Teacher induction and mentoring: School-based collaborative programs.* Albany, NY: SUNY Press.

Mager, G. (In press). The place of induction in becoming a teacher. In G. DeBolt, ed., *Teacher induction and mentoring: School-based collaborative programs.* Albany, NY: SUNY Press.

McKenna, G. (1988). *Analysis of the benefits of being a mentor in a formal induction program.* Unpublished dissertation, Loyola University of Chicago.

Odell, S.; and Ferraro, D. (In press). Collaborative teacher induction. In G. DeBolt, ed., *Teacher induction and mentoring: School-based collaborative programs.* Albany, NY: SUNY Press.

Taharally, C.; Gamble, M.; and Marsa, S. (In press). The dynamics of professional collaborative relationships in a mentoring program in selected New York City elementary schools. In G. DeBolt, ed., *Teacher induction and mentoring: School-based collaborative programs.* Albany, NY: SUNY Press.

Wolfe, M.; and Stupiansky, N. (In press). The North Country mentor/intern teacher program. In G. DeBolt, ed. *Teacher induction and mentoring: School-based collaborative programs.* Albany, NY: SUNY Press.

Index